THE CRO'S GUIDE TO WINNING IN PRIVATE EQUITY

THE CRO'S GUIDE TO WINNING IN PRIVATE EQUITY

A Practical Roadmap for Sales Leaders

JD MILLER, PhD

Advance Praise for
"The CRO's Guide to Winning in Private Equity"

The value creation playbook for CROs working in high-growth companies. JD Miller's expertise will accelerate results and improve the odds of beating your number.

Kevin Knieriem, GTM President, Clari

An essential guide that translates the language of private equity into actionable strategies for revenue leaders. JD has distilled over 20 years of experience into battle tested frameworks that will drive increased revenue visibility and growth.

Sim Allan, Principal, GrowthCurve Capital

JD Miller is one of few GTM leaders who understands how to masterfully blend commercial strategy with repeatable field execution in a private equity environment. His skill set of building and running an organic growth engine to new levels of scale is a rarity in today's selling environment.

Matt Sharrers, Executive Chairman, SBI: The Growth Advisory

Most sales leadership advice consists of fluffy nonsense like "it's all about the people." JD is a seasoned operator that has seen scale, but is able to get into the weeds on forecasting, territory planning, compensation plan design, and everything else I wish I had as a first-time VP of Sales.

Armand Farrokh, Founder of 30 Minutes to President's Club and Bestselling Author of Cold Calling Sucks (And That's Why It Works)

Until you are in the CRO seat, you will never understand it ... unless someone writes a behind-the-scenes book that gives you a firsthand look. JD Miller's CRO's Guide gives any current or future CRO an inside track on how a true professional runs their shop.

Mark Kosoglow, CEO, Operator

This book unlocks the full potential of the CRO role, transforming it from a sales leader to a true strategic partner. A powerful resource for both executives and boards.

Craig Powell, multi-time CEO and Board Director

A CRO's perspective on driving revenue growth in partnership with their key stakeholders, specifically owners and investors. This book provides a blueprint for the key metrics and strategies that matter.

Richard Hogg, CEO, Vizibl

A practical and insightful playbook for any operator stepping into a CRO role. This book will help you hit the ground running and deliver the impact your investors expect. This book was invaluable so that I could come up to speed quickly for my first experience in the private equity world.

David Harris, Senior VP of Sales, Springbrook Software

"The CRO's Guide to Winning in Private Equity" should be required reading for any CRO working with a PE firm. It demystifies the partnership and provides the tools for achieving rapid, sustainable growth.

Ryan Fast, Chief Revenue Officer, n2y

A roadmap to bridge the gap between strategic vision and bottom-line results, "The CRO's Guide to Winning in Private Equity" is an invaluable asset for any growth-minded company, PE-owned or not.

Tony Erickson, Senior Partner, SBI: The Growth Advisory

A must-read for any CRO in the PE- or VC-backed world. This isn't theory: It's hard-won experience - turned into a battle-tested playbook for building value. Every CRO should have this book on their desk.

David Farquhar, Serial Entrepreneur and Entrepreneur-in-Residence @The University of Edinburgh

A must-read for any leader looking to accomplish predictable, time-bound revenue growth.

Aaron Campbell, Managing Partner, Operation Autopilot

This book isn't just about sales; it's about operational excellence. Miller provides a clear, strategic framework that aligns sales with the broader goals of their company.

Jack Debono, Head of Community, Revenue Operations Alliance

JD's approach to aligning sales and marketing is both practical and insightful - and the partnership drives results. "The CRO's Guide to Winning in Private Equity" should be required reading for any leader looking to build a high-performing, collaborative team.

Tim Fitzgerald, CMO, Tripleseat

"War is a science, with rules to be applied."

~ Charlemagne/Stephen Schwartz, Pippin

Table of Contents

Introduction

I never intended to work in sales.

Despite the freshman convocation speaker's prediction that 75% of my incoming class at the University of Illinois would be working in "jobs that didn't even exist yet" when we graduated because of the newly-created Internet, most of my high school classmates assumed that we'd wind up in one of three careers: engineer, doctor or—my choice—lawyer. A double major in Philosophy and Communication joined a minor in Comparative Literature to create a pre-law curriculum of thinking, speaking, and writing.

When an internship in the Clinton White House changed my mind about going to law school, I suddenly needed to re-evaluate my options. There didn't seem to be many jobs for professional philosophers, or literature comparers, either. My communication degree seemed the most promising, and an offer to work in a research lab studying the ways the communication networks we understood in the physical world translated to this Internet-enabled one kept me on campus for another year to work on a master's degree and the start of my PhD.

True to the convocation speaker's prediction, the early 2000s arrived and my never-heard-of-before degree in online social networks brought a number of dot-com companies calling. I accepted a job as a Solutions Engineer, demonstrating how software could be used to create and manage the first websites of Fortune 100 companies who were just learning how call centers, marketing initiatives, and sales experiences might be transformed online. They were great years to be in tech sales, and whether we were lucky or good, our company went from having 26 employees to 6,000 in a few years, trading on the stock exchange as one of the largest tech IPOs until Google's legendary market debut eclipsed us.

As I completed my dissertation, writing about this new frontier of online communication, my academic training also made me realize that a lot of what we think of as "the art of sales" is actually much more scientific. Groups make decisions in predictable ways that are driven by predictable influences. While the biggest deals are often sold to companies with over a dozen decision-makers involved in evaluating and selecting new products, great sales organizations can train their sellers to use a scientific understanding of these processes to influence the chance of a win.

Twenty-some years later, I've been through a number of mergers and acquisitions backed by a variety of private equity firms. I've also risen through the ranks from individual contributor to executive, having held roles as quota-carrying seller, CRO, country CEO, and a variety of roles in between.

Through it all, I've learned a fundamental truth: sales and marketing can be guided toward consistent wins. It's the core of my work today as an operating advisor to PE firms and their portfolios, honing a strategic playbook that gives our companies a competitive advantage in their pursuit of stronger returns.

This book reveals that playbook.

Consider this a field guide for the modern CRO. It distills decades of hard-won knowledge, aiming to make your path smoother and your results more impactful.

While my background lies in the specific niche of global B2B tech and tech-enabled services, particularly with companies in the $50M to $300M revenue range who are owned by a private equity firm, I believe the core principles within these pages hold valuable lessons for a wide variety of businesses.

The chapters unfold chronologically, mirroring a year in the life of your business. You'll move from strategic planning to the nitty-gritty of the daily, weekly, monthly, and quarterly routines that make those plans a reality. I've shared examples of templates and tools for various processes that you can put to use today, as well as chapters on essential topics like collaborating with cross-functional teams and engaging effectively with your PE partners and board. I've included links to bonus materials and templates that you can download and put into immediate use in order to make this book your indispensable companion as a modern CRO.

Happy selling.

CHAPTER 1
Setting the Annual Plan

The first time I carried a quota, I had no idea where it came from. It was $1.2M, and I had a rough idea that if I could sell a single $100k deal every month, I'd finish the year at plan. I did, and the next year I received a 33% increase in my target. How annoying! But I achieved it, and the next year, my quota increased to $2.5M, more than twice the quota I had in my first year of selling!

I hit that, too, but thought my management team was getting greedy. Our list price had increased quite a bit in the previous two years. I was getting those deals done, but I was wondering how much further management was going to push things before the price got too high for me to be able to sell anything. My deals were closing faster, and I was averaging three new deals every two months. Each audacious new goal was achieved and beaten, but I wasn't sure if that was by luck or because I was becoming a better seller with three whole years of experience.

My pessimistic peers looked at these goals—twice what they were when we were hired!—and assumed that our pre-IPO company was trying to minimize expenses by creating quotas that would come with lower commission rates. They grumbled about having to do twice the amount of work to earn the same commission they'd had two years before.

In retrospect, there was probably some truth in all of it.

Sitting on the other side of the table, setting quotas every year as CRO, I know that multiple factors come into play, including the size of the market opportunity, the cost of sale, and a hard-to-define measure of

"How far can I push my teams without destroying our culture and morale?" that comes from analyzing prior performance data and my interaction with sellers on the front lines each day.

As I've played this role over the years, I've come to believe that the work of setting the annual plan is the most important work a sales leader does all year long to create a high-performing team. When we get it right, we set our teams up for a year of success and exceeded expectations. Sellers earn great commission checks, and the culture of winning is one everyone wants to be a part of. Almost nobody leaves the company, and we're able to recruit more people to join us because word on the street is that we're a great place to work.

When we get the annual plan wrong, we're locked in a constant struggle, scrambling to make up for missed targets and cutting costs in response. The most talented sellers quickly leave for jobs where they think they'll succeed, and we struggle to recruit new talent because they hear rumors that nobody is making quota at our company.

One of my most miserable years as a leader was when I knew early on that we'd set a plan we couldn't achieve. Poor planning gave me a grinding year with pressure from a CEO who expected me to pull bluebirds and sales rabbits out of magic hats daily. My CFO wanted to cut costs to adjust for the missed revenue expectations but thought we should still chase the same annual target, even as we reduced the size of my struggling sales teams. Employees laid off from other departments blamed my team's lack of sales for their lost jobs and took to sites like Glassdoor to publicly share criticism of me by name.

The board asked every few days about how much longer we'd have to wait to see things turn around, offering well-intentioned suggestions about what we could do differently tomorrow to get a better result than what we had today. I had to put all that negative emotion aside to stand before my team each day and convince them that brighter days were ahead. All the while, praying desperately that disillusioned sellers wouldn't leave for better pastures and leave me with newer, un-ramped sellers who were even less likely to achieve our unattainable goals.

It's an experience no sales leader wants to have. Yet, as important as the annual plan is to our personal happiness and our companies' success, many CROs have no idea how to do it well, and several stumble on this high-stakes task.

Over the years, I've seen some, let's call them, 'creative' approaches to setting quotas and targets. Perhaps you've worked with a leader or two who built an optimistic plan in similar ways:

- The CEO who grudgingly signed off on a two-day sales training program and then declared that each seller should be at least 5% better as a result, raising the sales target 5% more the following year based solely on that investment.

- The VP of Sales who decided that closing "just one more deal" per seller was the magic formula for success. They happily accepted a target that depended on it happening and sent an email to the team telling them to dig deeper to find an extra deal in each territory, but had no real plan for how or where those incremental deals would materialize.

- The CEO who was in love with the 31% super-accelerator commission plan that he created. His assumption was that our sellers just needed more motivation to unlock hidden potential in the market. "I don't understand what's wrong," he'd say, "don't they realize how much money they'd make if they could sell a million dollars more?" Spoiler alert: the market didn't have a million dollars of extra opportunity hiding in anyone's territory, and nobody ever got paid out 31% in the years that "plan" was in place.

- Perhaps my favorite was the VP who vowed zero tolerance for underperformance and built a plan that assumed 100% quota attainment from every seller every month of the year. She led with an iron fist, threatening to fire any sellers who couldn't achieve the plan. The top performers, of course, quickly found new jobs at companies with better cultures, leaving an impossible-to-fill quota gap in their wake for the months it took to recruit and train sellers to backfill their roles. Perhaps learning from this mistake, the VP adjusted the following year by signing up for a target that was another 10% higher, passing out 10% increases in quota for all sellers, but also "hiring one or two extra reps, just for cushion."

With such flawed thinking, is it any surprise that a QuotaPath study determined that 91% of sales teams miss their annual targets?

While many boards and CFOs will sign off on plans built on flawed assumptions like these, the challenge is that they're often not backed up with real plans to get there. Pretty early in the year, the team starts missing these sales targets and then plays catchup for the rest of the year, taking increasingly drastic measures to try and course correct as the gap to meeting the plan widens. The course corrections aren't pretty. Unreasonable expectations set the organization up for missed numbers, which leads to a lack of confidence in the team and increased scrutiny and pressure to "catch up the miss" with even more unreasonable goals. I've lived the cycle once or twice in my own career and know that nobody is happy—not me, not my sellers, not my executive team, and not my board—as we churn through never-ending conversations about what is going wrong.

I hate working in that environment.

That's why I've become obsessively unwaveringly focused on building an annual plan that I can achieve. I make sure every member of my executive team and board understands each assumption we've made about "what has to go right" to hit the plan we've laid out, and I don't let the conversation go until we're all completely aligned.

At times, it's tedious. Colleagues ask, "Can't we just count on a surprise $500k from something good this year?" However, staying engaged in these difficult conversations at the start of the year increases the probability that we won't have to have even more agonizing ones for the 12 months we're actually executing against the plan and assigned quotas.

I'm not exactly popular when we're having these conversations, but they do result in a plan rooted in realistic, appropriate, and well-understood expectations by my entire leadership team. Once we've built a good plan that the company is likely to achieve, I use it to set appropriate quotas for my sellers, and I understand that the company's sales target and the total quota on the street are not the same.

Ready to learn my approach? It follows a few key steps.

Understanding Your Growth Target

Every company I've worked for wants to grow. When they've recruited me, they've been able to clearly identify a number—say 20%—that they want to grow by year-over-year. More specifically, the tech companies I've worked for set targets for the growth of their Annual Recurring Revenue (ARR). This is the measure of the predictable, recurring revenue generated from subscriptions to the software products we sell across a one-year period. Measuring a company's ARR is a key piece of valuing the company determining the price a PE firm will pay to buy it. Non-recurring charges like setup fees, professional services, hardware sales, or consulting fees are not included in ARR.

Yet, knowing that you're tasked with growing ARR 20% alone isn't enough to understand how challenging your job will be as the CRO. Factors like customer satisfaction, the overall health of the business, and the overall expansion or contraction of the economy you're operating in can make that task easier or harder before you've ever spoken with a new customer. PE firms regularly track "Gross Retention" and "Net Retention" calculations as a shorthand for those metrics and monitor them closely because they have a direct impact on how easy (or hard) it will be to achieve annual growth targets going forward.

Take, for example, a company with customers who have bought annual subscriptions to their products that total $100M. This company starts the year with $100M of ARR. The gross retention rate is calculated by dividing the ARR the company finishes the year with after each customer has renewed (or not renewed) their subscription for the next year by this starting $100M. If, over the course of the year, the company fails to renew $5M of its customers' subscriptions, the company's gross retention is 95%.

Gross retention measures the "stickiness" of the company's products and the effectiveness of its organization in preventing churn. It does not include expansion revenue from upsells, cross-sells, or price increases. Those are included in net retention calculations, which indicate the company's ability to retain customers and grow revenue from them.

If, for example, the company began the year with a set of customers who spent $100M in ARR and finished the year with those same customers spending $107M in ARR, their net retention is 107%. The net retention metric is a key influencer of how easy or hard it will be for the company to achieve its annual plan. If our example company intends to grow 20% year over year, its strong 107% net retention rate means that the sales team will only need to sell an incremental $13M of new business ARR to achieve its goal.

120% Growth With Positive Net Retention

Increase ⬜ Decrease ⬛ Total

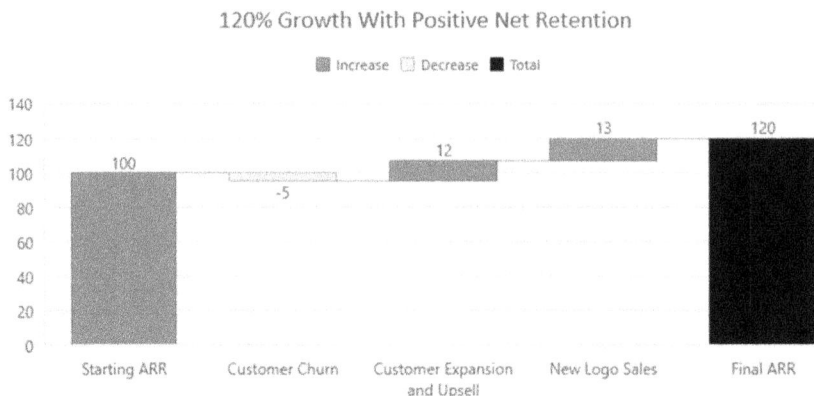

Fig 1.1: Strong Net Retention Relieves Pressure on New Logo Sales

Poor net retention would make things much harder. Consider the same 20% growth target in a scenario where the company has a net retention of only 85%. Their sales team will first have to sell $15M of new business to simply break even year to year and then have to sell an additional $20M of new business to meet the ARR target for the year. Since it's generally considered much harder and more expensive to win a new customer than retain or upsell an existing one, this company has a much harder road ahead of it to get to the same annual growth result. The scenario where they start with poor net retention requires more than two and a half times the new logo deals needed to get the same result they would have achieved under the better net retention scenario.

I learned this lesson the hard way when I took a job without asking about the existing net retention of the business. A few weeks into the job, I learned there was a huge "leaky bucket" of churning revenue from unhappy customers, leaving me the dual task of getting intimately involved as an executive sponsor to clients in order to prevent losing them and running a bigger-than-expected campaign to win new logos, too.

120% Growth With Negative Net Retention

■ Increase □ Decrease ■ Total

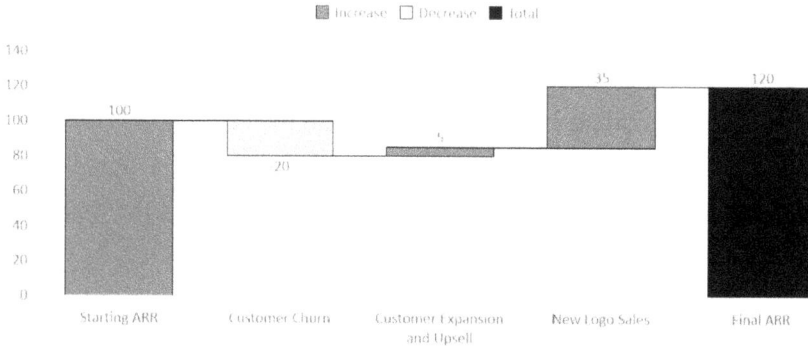

Fig 1.2: Poor Net Retention Increases Pressure on New Logo Sales

You'd better believe that net retention is now one of the first things I look at every time I evaluate a new opportunity. I highly prefer companies with strong net retention rates because they're easier places to achieve my targets and earn my bonuses.

For many of the same reasons, gross and net retention are on the top of the list of things to check out for private equity investors. They may look for different targets based on the company's overall maturity, the types of customers they sell to, and their product prices. In the B2B SaaS companies I've worked with, a gross retention rate of 90-95% is usually considered "good," as is a net retention greater than 100%.

These targets recognize that some of your customers will go out of business, or there will be valid reasons why you'll be unable to hold on to every one of them, but you'll still be able to grow year-over-year revenue from the install base. Maintaining retention rates in these ranges makes your company one that is growing before you've gone through the time, effort, and expense of winning a single new customer.

Model Your Existing Customer Business

Given the impact that customer retention can have on overall success, the first step in my annual planning process is to model my existing business. My sales career has been spent in B2B tech companies that tend to sell multi-year contracts to corporate customers. The agreements include language around annual price increases and terms for renewing or canceling contracts after a predefined period.

When I've driven my teams to sell contracts with a three-to-five-year term, it has meant that I can start each year with a lot of my ARR goal "done," as most contracts aren't up for renewal in any given year. So, the first step of my annual plan is to look at which contracts will be up for renewal in the coming year, the customer satisfaction rate, and what price increases have already been agreed to in the contract.

Ideally, you will have a software system that tracks this for you, but for example purposes, let's look at a spreadsheet that describes the details of customers who are up for renewal in the first few months of the year. Specifically, we're looking at the date their contract should renew, any price increases the renewal allows, their current satisfaction level, and whether their contract indicates that the renewal will be for a single year or a multi-year term:

Customer	Renewal Date	Increase Allowed	Satisfaction	Multi-Year
Apex Zenith Group	JAN	2%	YELLOW	NO
NovaWave	FEB		GREEN	NO
Stellar Synergy	FEB	2%	GREEN	YES
LuminaCore	MAR	6%	GREEN	YES
Quantum Innovations	MAR	0%	GREEN	YES
Veridian	APR	2%	RED	YES
Ethos	APR		GREEN	YES
TerraForge	MAY		YELLOW	YES
Chronosync Tech	MAY	7%	YELLOW	YES

Fig 1.3: A List of Customers up for Renewal with Descriptions of Their Contracted Terms

From here, you can create a strategy for how to treat each renewal. In this example, you might prioritize renewal negotiations that get each customer locked into a three-year term, as a potential PE buyer of the company will want to know how much revenue is "locked up" for the first few years following their purchase. Contracted price increases will represent locked-in growth, so you might work to get some price increase language into any multi-year contracts that don't already have it.

You might assume that happy (green-status) customers will bear a 5% price increase but settle on a 2% renewal in exchange for a multi-year agreement during negotiation. In this hypothetical example, LuminaCore is a happy customer whose contract calls for a 6% increase on a multi-year renewal, so you might plan on that happening as contracted.

For the yellow-status customers, you might be willing to forgo any price increase at all to get these on-the-fence customers locked into multi-year agreements. In this plan, then, you might not hold Chronosync to their contracted 7% increase. Instead, you might assume that the relationship, though yellow status, is strong enough that you can get half that increase and that they would appreciate the discount from their obligation of 7% as a show of goodwill on your part.

You might also assume that red-status customers will not renew.

The companies I've worked for sell their products "per user, per year," and so they also enjoy some organic expansion from customers calling to say they've hired new employees and need to purchase additional licenses to cover them. I look to historic trends to estimate that growth and incorporate it into my plans.

With all of these factors in mind, you can create a month-by-month expectation of revenue coming from your install base, though you will also plan for cross-selling new products to these customers as part of your "new business" plan later. While a real annual plan would be for the entire year, this example shows just the first few months and has calculated gross and net retention on just the data shown here:

Customer	Increase Allowed	Satisfaction	Multi-Year	JAN	FEB	MAR	APR	MAY	STRATEGY
Apex Zenith Group	2%	YELLOW	NO	$ 44,516.00					Multi-year with 0%
NovaWave		GREEN	NO		$276,430.00				Multi-year with 2%
Stellar Synergy	2%	GREEN	YES		$ 15,796.00				2%
LuminaCore	6%	GREEN	YES			$589,478.00			6%
Quantum Innovations	0%	GREEN	YES			$138,574.00			0%
Veridian	2%	RED	YES				$310,176.00		Churn
Ethos		GREEN	YES				$115,239.00		5%
TerraForge		YELLOW	YES					$568,656.00	Multi-year with 0%
Chronosync Tech	7%	YELLOW	YES					$216,118.00	3.50%

	JAN	FEB	MAR	APR	MAY	TOTALS
UP-FOR-RENEAL	$ 44,516.00	$292,226.00	$728,052.00	$425,415.00	$ 784,774.00	$ 2,274,983.00
RENEWED REVENUE	$ 44,516.00	$292,226.00	$728,052.00	$115,239.00	$ 784,774.00	$ 1,964,807.00
PRICE INCREASE		$ 5,844.52	$ 35,368.68	$ 5,761.95	$ 7,564.13	$ 54,539.28
ORGANIC EXPANSION	$ 22,976.00	$ 7,180.00	$ -	$ -	$ 61,030.00	$ 91,186.00
INSTALL BASE PLAN	$ 67,492.00	$305,250.52	$763,420.68	$121,000.95	$ 853,368.13	$ 2,110,532.28

GROSS RETENTION	86%
NET RETENTION	93%

Fig 1.4: Translating Customer Health and Renewal Terms into a Monthly Revenue Plan

Use Historical Performance Data To Shape Future New Business Expectations

Once I understand the revenue from my existing customers, the next step is to create a plan for new business throughout the year. My academic background tells me that past performance is generally the best indicator of future performance. So, when I want to know what a new business team is going to do next year, I start by taking a look at what they did this year and the year before.

As CRO, you'll definitely work on better sales messaging, putting your sellers through training programs, and launching better products. Still, it's important that you take a conservative view, grounded in realistic expectations, when you account for the impact those actions will have and on what time horizon.

To set a team's baseline expectation of performance, I start by looking at a few metrics:

- For sellers that have been around a while: What has their average booking been by month, quarter, and year?

- For new sellers: How many months did it take for them to get their first sale? How long did it take until their sales volume matched that of the tenured sellers? What was their monthly performance across this onboarding period?

With these questions answered you can start building a month-by-month spreadsheet that includes each of your team members, where they are in their ramping period, and what their expected bookings should be. Here's an example of a sales team with four fully ramped sellers and three in various stages of onboarding at a company where new hires take six months to get to a fully ramped bookings run rate.

	JAN	FEB	MAR	APR	MAY	JUN	JUL
Arianna Garnett	Full Performance	Full Performance	Full Performance	Full Performance	Full Performance	Full Performance	Full Performance
Callan Herriot	Full Performance	Full Performance	Full Performance	Full Performance	Full Performance	Full Performance	Full Performance
Jake Weaver	Full Performance	Full Performance	Full Performance	Full Performance	Full Performance	Full Performance	Full Performance
Kyle York	Full Performance	Full Performance	Full Performance	Full Performance	Full Performance	Full Performance	Full Performance
Rose Underwood	Month 1 Ramp	Month 2 Ramp	Month 3 Ramp	Month 4 Ramp	Month 5 Ramp	Full Performance	Full Performance
Janae Walton	Month 4 Ramp	Month 5 Ramp	Full Performance	Full Performance	Full Performance	Full Performance	Full Performance
Rex Osbourne	Month 3 Ramp	Month 4 Ramp	Month 5 Ramp	Full Performance	Full Performance	Full Performance	Full Performance

Fig 1.5: A list of Sellers with Various Tenures and Their Revenue Production Expectations by Month

Consider Turnover

Next, I think about what turnover on my team will look like in the coming year. Sure, we're a great place to work, but people get married, have kids, or simply decide to leave for other opportunities.

I will also choose to let some poor performers go, and these need to be planned for, too. As I work on this part of the plan, I ask myself:

- What has turnover been like over the past year or two?

- Are there individuals I already know will exit in the coming year, by my choice or theirs?

- Are there particular times of year when I think this will happen?

- How long does our recruiting process take to replace a quota carrier who's left the organization?

Each answer will have an implication for the amount of quota I can reliably have on the street and, by extension, how much revenue to expect to be sold in a given territory. Once you have made it to this point, you can add rows into your spreadsheet to represent the loss of quota for anticipated turnover and the ramping quotas (post-recruiting lag) for their replacement.

In practice, I find that most sellers who are going to leave the organization start thinking about it in the fourth quarter. They do some interviewing, see what the new comp plan looks like at the start of the next year, wait for the payment of their last commissions/annual bonuses, and then resign. The best organizations anticipate this and are already conducting exploratory interviews with sales candidates before a resignation is accepted. However, for planning purposes, you shouldn't expect to have an immediate replacement waiting in the wings.

With that in mind, here's an example of how you might model the loss of one fully-ramped seller on January 31st and a replacement being found 60 days later:

	JAN	FEB	MAR	APR	MAY	JUN	JUL
Arianna Garnett	Full Performance	Full Performance	Full Performance	Full Performance	Full Performance	Full Performance	Full Performance
Callan Herriot	Full Performance	Full Performance	Full Performance	Full Performance	Full Performance	Full Performance	Full Performance
Jake Weaver	Full Performance	Full Performance	Full Performance	Full Performance	Full Performance	Full Performance	Full Performance
Kyle York	Full Performance	Full Performance	Full Performance	Full Performance	Full Performance	Full Performance	Full Performance
Rose Underwood	Month 1 Ramp	Month 2 Ramp	Month 3 Ramp	Month 4 Ramp	Month 5 Ramp	Full Performance	Full Performance
Janae Walton	Month 4 Ramp	Month 5 Ramp	Full Performance	Full Performance	Full Performance	Full Performance	Full Performance
Rex Osbourne	Month 3 Ramp	Month 4 Ramp	Month 5 Ramp	Full Performance	Full Performance	Full Performance	Full Performance
TURNOVER REPLACEMENT		Subtract Full Perf.	Subtract Full Perf.	Subtract Full Perf. Month 1 Ramp	Subtract Full Perf. Month 2 Ramp	Subtract Full Perf. Month 3 Ramp	Subtract Full Perf. Month 4 Ramp
Baseline Expectation	SUM ABOVE	SUM ABOVE	SUM ABOVE	SUM ABOVE	SUM ABOVE	SUM ABOVE	SUM ABOVE

Fig 1.6: Accounting for Seller Turnover in Revenue Planning

18

Make Strategic Adjustments

At this point, I sum each of the columns and get a pretty strong sense of what revenue generation will look like for each month of the year. This is the baseline bookings expectation. Next, I compare that baseline number to my leadership team's desired targets.

Most private equity-backed companies are working to become "Rule of 40" investments and set booking targets accordingly. The "Rule of" calculation represents how well the company is balancing growth and profitability and is derived by adding the percentage of annual growth to the percentage of annual profit, measured by EBITDA: earnings before interest, taxes, depreciation, and amortization.

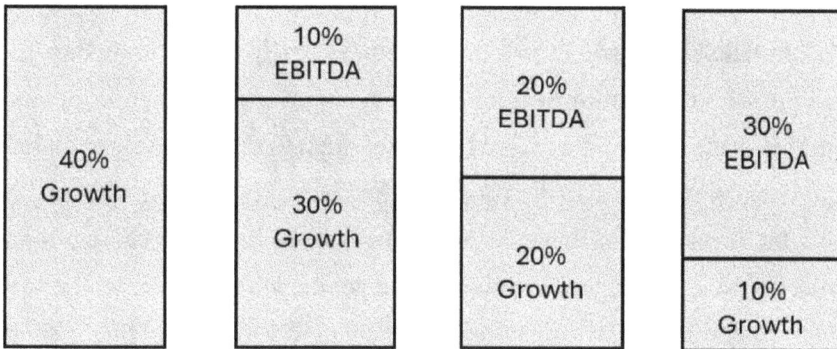

Fig 1.7: Some Ways to Balance Growth and Profitability in a "Rule of 40" Company

There are many ways for companies to achieve the Rule of 40. They might be growing at 50% but losing 10% of profit annually. They might be growing 10% and running a business with 30% EBITDA. They may be balanced with 20% growth and 20% profit.

In different investing environments, there may be different preferences for how the Rule of 40 is achieved. During the dot-com boom, the mantra was "growth at all costs," and investors gladly took negative profitability for a few years if it meant that companies were snapping up market share with high growth rates. Recently, there's been a preference for investing in companies that have at least break-even or positive EBITDA in the calculation and, within those bounds, a preference for more growth than EBITDA if possible.

No matter how they get there, though, a company that can find any way to achieve Rule of 40 will get higher prices when sold to the next investor than a company that can't. Achieving an annual plan that results in a Rule of 40 (or better!) means more money for the PE firm, more money for your board, more money for you, and a sterling credential for your resume.

Straight talk: Unless you're working for an extremely unique company, the baseline sales expectation you had by carrying prior performance forward into this year's plan isn't going to be high enough to achieve the growth rate your particular Rule of 40 plan is calling for. Most PE firms buy things that are a bit "broken" and have an investment thesis that they can fix some structural things to make them better and get a higher price when they do. Well-run companies who are already achieving Rule of 40 don't necessarily meet that goal, so your run rate probably has room for improvement.

Assuming the baseline plan you've built doesn't show the growth that your board wants to see, you need to think about what strategic actions you can take in the year to close the gap.

- Can you add additional headcount? How many and in what timeframe? Model additional ramping sellers into your plan (as long as you're confident you have enough territory in your total addressable market that they won't cannibalize the performance of your existing team).

- Are you launching a new marketing or training program that can raise performance? Figure out in what month the impact would be expected, and increase the monthly performance by the appropriate percentage from that point forward.

- Are you bringing new products to market? When will they be ready to sell, and how long will it take to book one, two, or ten deals that include them?

Each of these strategies will have cost implications, and you'll need to work closely with the rest of the organization to ensure that you're all aligned on how Rule of 40 is impacted by any of them.

Perhaps you're working with a huge Total Addressable Market (TAM), and your current sales team isn't big enough to capture it all. You might determine that there's enough room to add 16 new sellers to the team. However, the cost of recruiting and hiring them (along with the supporting managers, solutions engineers, and marketing spend to make them successful) might not be recouped by their sales in their first year, since there's often a performance ramping period before a new seller is fully trained and effective. This strategy might have a short-term negative impact on EBITDA that would have to be balanced on the hope that there will be much more growth in future years. Or, perhaps you've decided that you'd produce more profit by reducing the size of your sales team and only going after the very largest target accounts, reducing the marketing spend and pursuit costs of trying to attract and win any small-to-medium-business opportunities.

As you evaluate these options, make sure everyone believes in the assumptions around their impact and timing on sales performance, and are committed to doing their part to support them. HR may need to commit to recruiting candidates within a particular time frame. Investments may need to be made in the engineering team to ensure that a new product offering will be in the market on a specific date. Finance, support, and operations teams may need to be prepared to deal with the implications that a de-investment in certain client segments may have on customer satisfaction and contract churn.

These discussions should be grounded in SMART objectives, ones that are Specific, Measurable, Achievable, Realistic, and Time-Bound. Consider an annual plan that anticipates significant growth from selling a soon-to-be-launched new product. Some questions to consider:

- Which specific accounts (or types of accounts) do we think this product will be sold to in the coming year? Are they already in our install base, or are they new logo opportunities? Which industries do we think these clients are in, and what business unit or decision maker will these products resonate with?

- How will we measure success on this initiative? How many new leads will we need to generate for this new product, and how many of those leads will have to buy it for it to be considered a success?

- Do we have the right access to lead lists, the right product collateral, and the right training materials for our sellers to make this strategy achievable?

- Is it realistic to believe that the first version of the product we launch will be full-featured enough to make it minimally viable in the market as an alternative to competitive offerings already in the space?

- Given our understanding of the length of our sales cycles, what are the dates we need to hit for seller training, pre-launch marketing, and product release date? How many deals need to include this product in each month of the year in order to achieve our plan?

SMART questioning can uncover the many ways that a plan that appears to work in an Excel spreadsheet may not work in reality. Mathematically, you might conclude that a company with 50 sellers may be able to achieve a particular growth goal by hiring 40 more. However, imagining the reality of that organization in six months when nearly 50% of every employee is brand new, the company may decide that they're not culturally prepared to welcome and train that many new people in the organization so quickly.

While the company's TAM analysis may conclude that there are more than enough prospects in a given geography to achieve a particular goal, those locations may not have a large enough talent pool to recruit from to pursue those opportunities. If there is enough available talent, HR may not have the capacity to move that many through the recruiting cycle in the time given without using an unbudgeted-for outside recruiter, or the training and onboarding of these sellers may require you to double the size of your sales enablement team before the work can begin.

When you and your executive team have aligned on all of these details, they're ready to be documented as discrete components of your annual plan. Figure 1.8 shows how the above assumptions might look in your hypothetical plan.

	JAN	FEB	MAR	APR	MAY	JUN	JUL
Arianna Garnett	Full Performance	Full Performance	Full Performance	Full Performance	Full Performance	Full Performance	Full Performance
Callan Henriot	Full Performance	Full Performance	Full Performance	Full Performance	Full Performance	Full Performance	Full Performance
Jake Weaver	Full Performance	Full Performance	Full Performance	Full Performance	Full Performance	Full Performance	Full Performance
Kyle York	Full Performance	Full Performance	Full Performance	Full Performance	Full Performance	Full Performance	Full Performance
Rose Underwood	Month 1 Ramp	Month 2 Ramp	Month 3 Ramp	Month 4 Ramp	Month 5 Ramp	Full Performance	Full Performance
Janae Walton	Month 4 Ramp	Month 5 Ramp	Full Performance	Full Performance	Full Performance	Full Performance	Full Performance
Rex Osbourne	Month 3 Ramp	Month 4 Ramp	Month 5 Ramp	Full Performance	Full Performance	Full Performance	Full Performance
TURNOVER		Subtract Full Perf.	Subtract Full Perf.	Subtract Full Perf.	Subtract Full Perf.	Subtract Full Perf.	Subtract Full Perf.
REPLACEMENT			Month 1 Ramp	Month 2 Ramp	Month 3 Ramp	Month 4 Ramp	Month 5 Ramp
Baseline Expectation	*SUM ABOVE*	*SUM ABOVE*	*SUM ABOVE*	*SUM ABOVE*	*SUM ABOVE*	*SUM ABOVE*	*SUM ABOVE*
INCREMENTAL IMPROVEMENTS							
TRAINING (training delivered)		*(no training impact)*	*Add 1% of above*	*Add 3% of above*	*Add 5% of above*	*Add 5% of above*	*Add 5% of above*
Q1 NEW HIRE	**Month 1 Ramp**	**Month 2 Ramp**	**Month 3 Ramp**	**Month 4 Ramp**	**Month 5 Ramp**	Full Performance	Full Performance
Q2 NEW HIRE				**Month 1 Ramp**	**Month 2 Ramp**	**Month 3 Ramp**	**Month 4 Ramp**
SELL NEW PRODUCT			Product Launch	Add 1 Sale	Add 1 Sale	Add 1 Sale	Add 1 Sale
FINAL SALES PLAN SUM ABOVE	*SUM ABOVE*	*SUM ABOVE*	*SUM ABOVE*	*SUM ABOVE*	*SUM ABOVE*	*SUM ABOVE*	*SUM ABOVE*

Fig 1.8: Accounting for Strategic Bets in Revenue Planning

In these moments, it's critical to remember that "Hope is not a plan." I once worked for an organization that was losing ground to a competitor but believed that launching a new feature set would improve our fortunes. Customers responded well to wireframe demos of what we were planning to build, and we signed off on an annual plan that depended on being able to sell it to them in June. Yet by the time March rolled around, disruptions in the development team meant the product wouldn't really be ready for release until sometime in September, and even then, only as a beta product for the smallest of accounts. The lead developers cheerfully shared plans that showed the enterprise-ready feature set would be available in January or February of the following year. It all added up to a scenario where very little of the product revenue we expected from this new release was going to be sellable or recognizable in the current year.

It's a real-world example that underscores an important rule: If your team is hoping that specific improvements will take shape without a tactical plan to ensure they happen, you should not model them into your annual plan, and you should not sign up for this increased sales goal. Only when your leadership team and board have committed to taking the appropriate steps should you add them to your annual plan, and you should label them to make it easy to track how future performance tracks to your planned assumptions.

If I hadn't done this, my board meetings would have devolved into rudimentary conversations that "the sales team is missing their annual target," and I'd have been battling all sorts of questions about the quality of my sellers, our sales process, or my leadership of the team. By building a plan that laid out specific revenue targets tied to each assumption, I could change the direction of meetings to ones that reported that "sellers are achieving their annual targets on all fronts except for sales of the new product. Unfortunately, that is no longer scheduled to be available this year, and we will not be able to deliver revenue against it through no fault of our own."

The reality is that missing targets "through no fault of our own" was still not acceptable, and I was still under pressure to find a way to plug that revenue gap in some way. Ultimately, I was able to cover part of the gap by overachieving in other elements of our plan, but still fell short of the year's overall revenue target. By helping everyone to realize why we landed on this result, I was seen as a hero who overcame adversity, rather than a villain who couldn't accomplish the expectations of my role.

That's a distinction that makes the difference between being a CRO your board trusts and wants to continue to invest in, and one they want to replace.

Use Quarterly Seasonality to Your Advantage

If you've followed each of the steps so far, you've got a realistic revenue plan to take you month by month through the year, and you've identified a foundation that clearly connects the needed investments in training, headcount, and new product to improved performance. You've also projected the timing implications of each of those strategic bets.

The final step of the planning process is to account for the seasonality of the business. So far, our calculations have assumed consistent performance from fully-ramped sellers across the year (so a tenured quota carrier with a $1.2M expectation would be delivering $100k every month). Yet, we know that most businesses have some sort of seasonality to them.

When I sold technology to retail companies, we knew that no new products would be implemented in the fourth quarter because they didn't want to undertake any projects that might disrupt their ability to keep stores running well during the holiday spending season. When I sold to accounting firms, I knew that very little would be sold in the first four months of the quarter since they were all heads-down on filing annual tax returns for their clients. When I sold CRM software, I saw a huge uptick in buyers wanting to have the product fully implemented by Q1 so they could launch it at their annual kickoff and deliver a solid year. Selling into the Italian market, I learned that most businesses more or less shut down in the third quarter as everyone in the country headed out for weeks-long seaside vacations.

Whatever drives your company's unique seasonality, it's helpful to look at your historical trends to figure out what percentage of your revenue happens in each quarter or each month, and then apply this shape to your final annual plan. Once you understand that, you can tweak your quarterly targets slightly to position your teams to overperform against expectations.

This is particularly important when I set first-quarter expectations, which I like to lower regardless of my company's seasonal history. Success builds on success, and teams perform best when they feel they're winning. It's also just more fun to be on a winning team than a losing one. That's why I like to lower the expectations for the first quarter of the year (making it up later on) so that my teams come out of the gates "beating the plan." In doing so, the morale of the team is much better than if they miss their first quarter and need to play catchup and deal with the cost-cutting measure that most CFOs will want to put in place as soon as they see a deviation from plan.

The other benefit to lowering first quarter expectations? You set yourself up as a leader who meets or beats expectations quarter after quarter, rather than one who misses all year long but manages to save it at the very end. This is a great professional brand. The adjustment doesn't need to be too big – just a few percentage points – to ensure the team meets or exceeds their Q1 plan. Here's an example of how a company's seasonality looked for the last two years and how I might tweak next year's plan to create a culture of winning:

	Q1	Q2	Q3	Q4
Last Year Actual	23%	20%	20%	37%
This Year Actual	24%	21%	20%	35%
Next Year Plan	20%	22%	22%	36%

Fig 1.9: Modeling the Quarterly "Shape" of a Sales Year

Based on the last two years' performance, this sales team should do 23% or 24% of their annual business in Q1. However, if I set the Q1 target at only 20%, they should finish that quarter ahead of plan. It's a team that has something to celebrate!

When I look to the end of Q2, previous performance would say this team will have retired 43-45% of the annual goal. In this plan, the expectation for the first half is only 42%, which should continue the culture of winning. They'll celebrate beating the first half goal!

In Q3, I've set expectations a bit higher but have banked some overperformance from prior quarters. History shows that this quarter will only do 20% of the year's revenue, and miss the 22% revenue target I've set here. However, the overperformance in the first half should still put them at 64% of plan, right in the middle of the 63% and 65% they did in prior years. The message to the team would be that we've slipped a little bit in this quarter but are still on track for our year-to-date performance. Let's rally together for a great end of year!

Finally, the 36% target for Q4 sits right in the middle of the 35% and 37% actuals in previous years. A safe bet to place for the final quarter of the year.

When Plans Meet Reality

There's a military saying that "No plan survives first contact with the enemy." We all know that a real sales year won't go perfectly according to the plan laid out on our nice spreadsheet. Nevertheless, I still believe that the plan I've built here gives us the best chance of success. It increases the odds of the sales leader having great news to report most of the time, which translates into great board meetings, less overall stress, and more job security.

Let's imagine a company that did $30M of new business last year, and $36M of new business this year—a 20% increase in performance. They've set an annual plan that includes further investment in sales and marketing that they think will result in 20% more improvement next year for a total of $43.2M, and they've spread the quarters as described in Figure 1.9. Let's assume that each quarter achieves the lowest percentage of growth from the prior two years (23% in Q1, 20% in Q2, 20% in Q3, and 35% in Q4). Here's how that performance might play out:

(in 000)	Q1	Q2	Q3	Q4	FY
Last Year Actual	$ 6.900	$ 6.000	$ 6.000	$ 11.100	$ 30.000
This Year Actual	$ 8.640	$ 7.560	$ 7.200	$ 12.600	$ 36.000
Next Year Plan	$ 8.640	$ 9.504	$ 9.504	$ 15.552	$ 43.200
YTD Plan	$ 8.640	$ 18.144	$ 27.648	$ 43.200	
Hypothetical NY Actual	$ 9.936	$ 8.640	$ 8.640	$ 15.120	$ 42.336
Q vs Plan	$ 1.296	$ (0.864)	$ (0.864)	$ (0.432)	
YTD vs. Plan	$ 1.296	$ 0.432	$ (0.432)	$ (0.864)	
% of Q Plan	115%	91%	91%	97%	
% of YTD Plan	115%	102%	98%	98%	
% of PYQ	115%	114%	120%	120%	
% of PYTD	115%	115%	116%	118%	

Fig 1.10: Performance Against Annual Plan Modeling Quarters of 20%, 22%, 22%, and 36%

There's no getting around the fact that this team will miss the plan if nothing changes. Taking the lesser quarterly performance percentage from the prior two years means, by definition, that they will hit less than 100% of this year's plan. But imagine how a year of quarterly board meetings will play out:

End of Q1

"Great News! We did 115% of our quarterly goal, and are ahead of plan by almost $1.3M."

End of Q2

"This quarter was softer than we'd planned for, but the overperformance in Q1 still puts us at 102% of our year-to-date goal and over-performing by more than $400k. That's 114% growth over Q2 of last year and 115% growth over the first half of last year."

End of Q3

"We saw a repeat of the softness from Q2. We really need to start digging in to understand if something has changed in our market, but we're still at 98% of our year-to-date goal. As a standalone quarter, we did 20% more than the same quarter last year. While we are behind plan by a little over $400k, we're at 116% of our performance in the first three quarters of last year. Looking at the pipeline for Q4, we don't see things falling apart in any major way next quarter."

End of Q4

"We saw a rebound from the last two quarters' misses. While we still didn't get to 100% of our quarterly plan, we came within 3% of it, falling short about $400k. Even better, we achieved 98% of our annual plan, which represents 18% growth year over year."

Now, let's consider the same actual sales performance in the context of a plan that expected the year to follow the exact same pattern as this year went (24% in Q1, 21% in Q2, 20% in Q3, and 35% in Q4):

(in 000)	Q1	Q2	Q3	Q4	FY
Last Year Actual	$ 6.900	$ 6.000	$ 6.000	$ 11.100	$ 30.000
This Year Actual	$ 8.640	$ 7.560	$ 7.200	$ 12.600	$ 36.000
Next Year Plan	$ 10.368	$ 9.072	$ 8.640	$ 15.120	$ 43.200
YTD Plan	$ 10.368	$ 19.440	$ 28.080	$ 43.200	
Hypothetical NY Actual	$ 9.936	$ 8.640	$ 8.640	$ 15.120	$ 42.336
Q vs Plan	$ (0.432)	$ (0.432)	$ -	$ -	
YTD vs. Plan	$ (0.432)	$ (0.864)	$ (0.864)	$ (0.864)	
% of Q Plan	96%	95%	100%	100%	
% of YTD Plan	96%	96%	97%	98%	
% of PYQ	115%	114%	120%	120%	
% of PYTD	115%	115%	116%	118%	

Fig 1.11: Performance Against Annual Plan Modeling Quarters of 24%, 21%, 20%, and 35%

Again, the same actual dollars would have been booked in each quarter, and you and your board might analyze what they mean in different ways. But I believe the narrative in each of these scenarios is less rosy:

End of Q1

"We got off to a slower start than expected and fell short of goal by a little over $400k. That's 15% better than Q1 of last year, but just 96% of our plan for the year. I know we just set this plan a few months ago, so this quarter should have been the easiest to predict, but we'll catch it up next quarter."

End of Q2

"We missed our Q2 by 5%, just a 1% bigger miss than in Q1. Even though this puts us at only 96% of our YTD plan, we are 15% better than we were at this point last year. We're $800k behind plan for the first half of the year, but I promise we are going to get to the bottom of things and straighten out performance next quarter."

End of Q3

"After missing plan the prior two quarters, we have now achieved 100% of the plan for Q3. We're still $800k behind the annual plan, but we didn't dig the hole any deeper. As a standalone quarter, Q3 is 120% of Q3 of last year and a 16% growth over year-to-date performance."

End of Q4

"Q4 represented two straight quarters of achieving 100% of the quarterly plan. As a standalone quarter, Q4 is 120% of Q4 last year. We kept our revenue shortfall to the 800k we had at the end of Q2 and Q3, and finished the year at 98% of plan, achieving 18% year over year growth."

Each board will vary, but in my experience, these narratives in which we are behind the YTD plan every quarter, elicit much more worry, anxiety, and discussion than the prior set which had us "ahead of plan" until the end of the third quarter, even when the full-year outcome is exactly the same.

Manage In-Quarter Seasonality Aggressively

If you are fortunate enough to have a board that only asks for performance data quarterly, congratulations! My own PE-backed boards have generally kept the four-hour marathon meetings to once a quarter, but they've also asked for at least a monthly checkpoint on sales progress. While boards understand that we can't be selling something every day, they do tend to get anxious to see tangible data to indicate that we're on track to meet or exceed our plan.

Yet, when I plot out the actual weekly bookings of companies I've seen, a typical quarter looks something like this:

Bookings Timing of $3,863,350

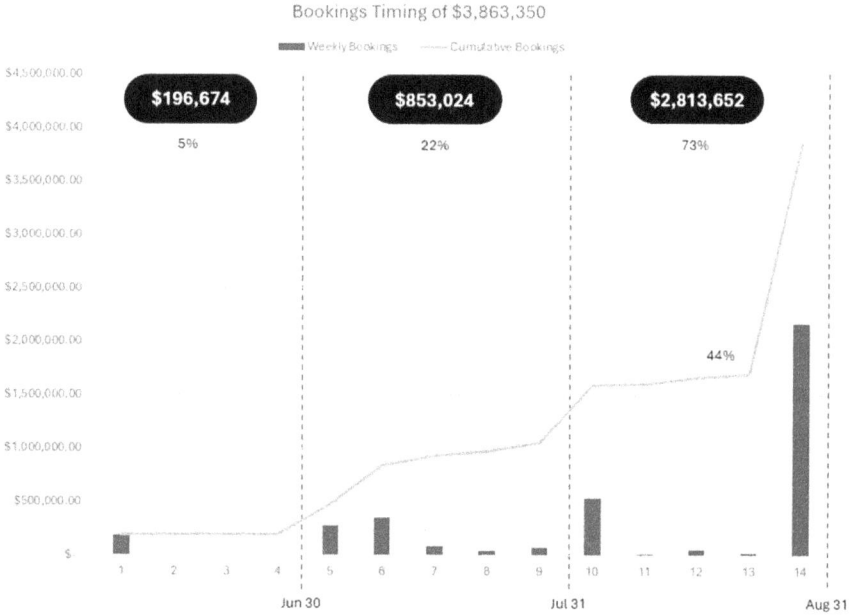

Fig 1.12: The Week-by-Week Shape of Most Companies' Sales Quarters

What do we see from this shape?

The team has a bit of activity in the first week of the quarter as they close out a handful of deals that slipped out of the prior quarter, and then the first month is pretty quiet. Things pick up a little bit in the second month but still only 27% of the quarter's goal has been hit by the end of the month. Urgency picks up in the final month, but one week before the quarter is over, only 44% of their deals have come in. More than half of the total revenue closes in the last seven days of this quarter.

Even if this team has achieved their financial plan for the quarter, it's a bit more of a… let's say, "thrilling" way to run a business than I like. When more than half of your deals close in a seven-day period, you're creating a really big backlog of work for the lawyers who need to redline contracts, services teams that need to negotiate scopes of work, and accounting teams that need to book deals and send invoices. Suppose your company is like most and operates on a calendar-based year. In that case, this also creates these end-of-quarter rushes around Christmas and New Year's vacations, the week before the Fourth of July, and that end-of-September time when back-to-school sports and activities are competing for attention.

While you may ultimately pull out a strong finish and hit your plan by the end of the quarter, you're only at 44% of the plan the week before the quarter ends. So, your CEO and board will be worried, calling you for daily updates and asking to inspect the close plans of every deal that might possibly still be winnable. It's a high-pressure situation that nobody wants. At the end of all of that anxiety, even when a team achieves its plan, nobody is going to feel great about how they got to that outcome, and you won't get the kudos you deserve. Most teams create urgency in their accounts by offering some sort of pricing discounts or compelling events to sign by a specific date, and most make those offers contingent on a close by the end of the month.

But what if we could just close deals on the 15th instead of the 30th?

There are usually a handful of deals that "slip" from one quarter to the next because the contract signer was out of the office, or the electronic signing process got delayed. Inevitably, you'll still extend the same concessions or discounts another week to the date they actually do sign. But when I've trained my teams to make their deals contingent on a close date of the 15th, those "slips" still have two full weeks to get closed and still count for my current quarter.

Here's a look at the impact of the same hypothetical company if they were successful in just closing 50% of their deals 15 days earlier than before, and moving those "first week of the quarter/slipped deals" back to the last week where they belong.

Bookings Timing of $3,863,350

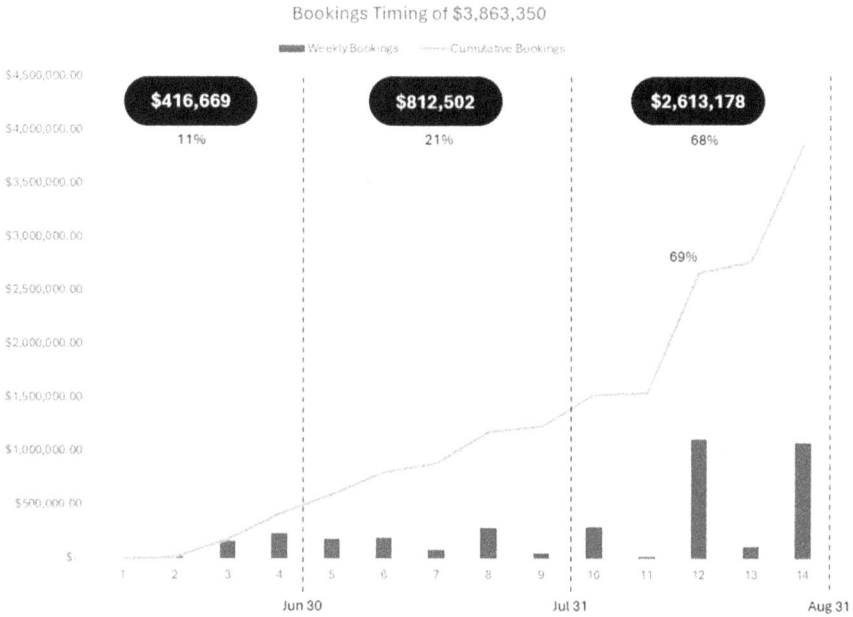

Fig 1.13: The Impact of Closing Half of the Deals 15 Days Earlier

That one small change made a huge difference. The team has almost 70% of the goal done with two entire selling weeks left in the quarter. It makes for a much less stressful culture for everyone involved.

I like to go one step further with my teams, though, and create special incentives for deals done in the first or second month of the quarter. I don't want it to be a financial incentive so that sellers don't have a reason to sandbag deals at the end of the quarter into the start of the next. Instead, I've had great success offering a "quick starters club" to any quota carrier who can get 66% of their quota retired by the end of the second month, rewarding them with some kind of trophy, recognition, or small overnight trip to celebrate over dinner as a group.

It's a big expectation to get all of our sellers to do this, and many won't. Still, look at what happens in our hypothetical quarter if only 25% of the sellers got two-thirds of their deals done in the first two months of the quarter, and half made their third-month deals happen on the 15th instead of the 30th:

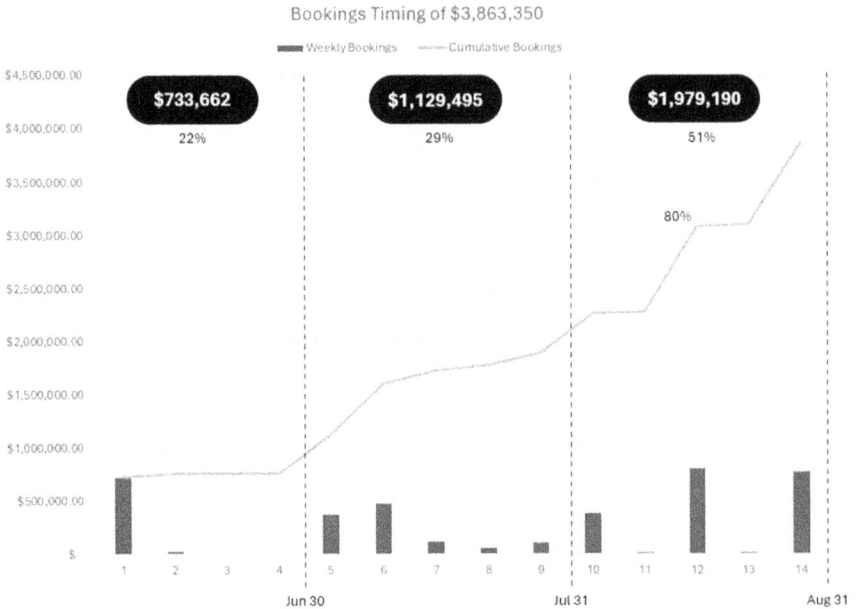

Fig 1.14: The Impact of Getting 25% of Sellers to Complete 66% of Their Quarterly Business by the Second Month.

Now we've gotten 80% of the quarter done with two selling weeks left. Even more comforting, we've really improved the performance in months one and two, entering the third month with over half of the number done. This is the kind of steady growth that gives you a reputation for being an even-keeled, steady sales leader.

Set Quotas

Now that you've built your annual plan, shaped seasonality appropriately, and gotten your management team's signoff on the key strategic bets involved, it's time to set quotas for the team. Many individual contributors—and a lot of first-time managers—assume that the plan you've been talking about and the assigned quota are the same thing. Yet a company that assumes every seller will achieve 100% of the quota assigned to them is destined to fail. No team is going to have perfect execution against plan across every seller, every month of the year. Sellers will leave the organization, territories will go empty for some periods of time, and life will intervene.

So far, our calculations have told us what the business should count on happening, but we want to motivate our teams to do a little bit more than this baseline expectation. My general rule of thumb is that you've got a happy sales team if 80% of your sellers are making between 80% and 100% of their quota, with a handful of folks overperforming significantly. I typically plan to make that happen by taking the expectations we've built and adding in a 15-20% cushion to these goals. I manage my sellers to this inflated quota rather than to the baseline revenue expectation in the business plan. My managers are aware of this inflation, and so I give them a bit of a break on their quotas, assigning something less than the sum of each of their individual team members' quotas.

Most businesses allocate 120% of the plan in quota to their sellers, 110% of the plan in quota to their front-line managers, and 105% of quota to their head of sales. I always try to negotiate that extra target out of my own compensation plan, so I'm tasked with the same goal as the business plan calls for. Similarly, the "management plan" of the business is a bit higher than the "Board Plan," a number you never talk about except in board meetings, which is even less aggressive a goal than you're managing your business to achieve.

The Takeaway

Get an Annual Planning Template at

https://bit.ly/4dTaUkq

Setting sales expectations and quotas with this process takes a little bit of work and a fair bit of familiarity with Excel or other data manipulation tools. But when it's done right, you're setting your management team's expectation of sales performance around a plan grounded in reality, with all of the implications of new hires, surprise terminations, seasonality, and other messiness that life brings.

You're also creating expectations for your sales team that encourage them to stretch just a little bit to put themselves (and you) in a place where you're always overperforming rather than falling short of expectations.

On a personal level, being the one who exceeds expectations consistently helps to create job security. It also positions your company for success – being surprised with a little bit of extra overperformance each month, and the option to invest it back into the business, rather than regularly falling slightly short and needing to make constant cost cuts instead.

That's a great way to run a business.

CHAPTER 2
Territory Planning and Quota Allocation

During one interview process, I kept hearing from a sales manager about how he recruited one of his best friends—we'll call him Ken—to join the team, and what a good decision that was because Ken was head and shoulders better than anyone else in the company. Ken had closed bigger dollar deals than any other seller but was a true team player. He'd retired over 200% of his quota but was humble about it. He was just an all-around nice guy. This was the profile of the seller we needed to hire going forward.

After taking the job, I made it a priority to meet with Ken right away. After talking with him for about 15 minutes, I have to say I was pretty unimpressed. He was, indeed, a nice guy who carried a conversation well, and he had an impressive list of big-dollar wins to his credit. Still, he couldn't really give me a terribly clear story about what our products did for our clients, nor could he really articulate anything about his sales process that was leading to success with them. "The product almost sells itself," he said humbly, continuing with praise for the rest of the team. "Our marketing team really does a great job identifying prospects, and our solutions engineers just come in with really smart demos that win the day. I just have to shepherd the process along and negotiate the contract."

My conversation with one of Ken's peers was a completely different story. Bright and articulate, this seller understood the market and taught me about our Ideal Customer Profile quickly. The peer followed a rigorous selling process too, but somehow wasn't putting up the numbers that Ken was. When asked, they had data to explain what was going on, which Ken's best friend/manager didn't want to address. The product was gaining traction in a particular industry that needed it more than anyone else and was willing to pay top dollar for it, too. The marketing team, in fact, had focused almost all of their efforts on cultivating this market and generated a lot of leads.

However, due to a geographic idiosyncrasy, it was an industry whose largest players were concentrated in one geographic region of the country. The territories they were working with put 90% of the best prospects in Ken's territory—more than he could even manage—while every other seller was struggling to cobble together a path to quota with much smaller accounts or prospects in less-lucrative industries.

When we re-balanced the territories to divide up these key accounts, everything about the team's performance changed. Suddenly, there were a lot of sellers achieving their quota, and they were winning deals in the target industry at higher average prices. Ken continued to win deals, but it was clear that he was consuming way more support resources than his peers, requiring more solutions engineering hours and executive sponsorship time to get deals over the line than anyone else on the team. As pressure ramped up on Ken and his manager to increase the efficiency of their sales process, both eventually left the company, and nobody seemed to miss them.

In Chapter 1, we spent time building out an annual sales plan that arrived at a revenue target based on a certain number of sellers achieving certain revenue targets each month of the year. While it will be rare to get there with every seller contributing equally every year, I spend a lot of time trying to set the table at the start of the year so everyone has an equal chance at doing so. My experience with Ken showed me that territory imbalances can mask a poor seller's deficiencies, or really handicap a strong one. So, the first step after building my annual plan is to balance territories that give everyone a fair playing field.

Separating New Logo, Install Base, and Renewal Teams

Most organizations have realized that there is a fundamentally different type of skill involved in selling to a completely new prospect than there is in selling to an existing customer. While there's a fair bit of overlap in general sales acumen, most sellers tend to gravitate towards one motion or the other, preferring the long-term relationship building of install-base sales or really thriving on the prospecting involved in new logo selling. Both types of selling are critical to your organization, but it's best to separate your "hunting sellers" from your "farming sellers" to maximize the usage of your teams' skills.

I've been surprised by how many companies I've consulted with who have not made that distinction. In particular, smaller, startup organizations or those with less than a dozen sellers seem to pursue a "double bag" approach that gives sellers a set of accounts to grow and renew, even as they are supposed to identify and win new logo deals.

When I dive into the performance data of these companies' teams, I find that they usually wind up with "hunters" and "farmers" in practice anyway. Many sellers spend most of their time and book almost all of their deals with install base accounts, while a smaller group really thrives at prospecting for and winning new business. Creating a separate team for each type of sale allows these sellers to maximize their productivity by focusing on the kinds of work they're great at, rather than giving partial attention to the kinds they're uninterested in.

There are also financial reasons that make it preferable to create separate hunting and farming teams. While it is hard to sell any product to anyone, sales to existing customers should be somewhat easier than new logo deals. Relationships are already built, trust in the company is already established, and so there should be less effort to get a current customer interested in a new product. This means that fewer marketing dollars will be spent on install base sales, and farming sellers can generally have lower base salaries and commission rates than their hunting peers.

When separating the New Logo and Install Base sales teams from one another, it is important to create a documented set of "rules of engagement" that establish which team gets credit for working with which customer at which point in time. New logo sellers will argue that it takes them a long time to get a prospect to make their first purchase with you, and they should be rewarded for sales to that customer for a long time. Install base sellers will be particularly concerned about credit for sales to accounts that failed to renew their contract, and then come back a very short time later for an additional purchase.

Your specifics will vary based on your product, typical contract length, and product offering, but a general set of rules that has worked for me has included:

- New logo sales get credit for any products purchased by the customer in their first year of the contract, including "effortless" upsell from the customer calling to request additional licenses for your product.

- Six months into the contract, the new logo seller should have opened an opportunity in the CRM system for any additional product sales they are actively working with the customer on evaluating.

- Between six and nine months into the contract, the new logo seller should introduce the install-base seller to the account as "their long-term account manager."

- Once introduced, the install base seller can actively start introducing any new products the new logo seller hasn't already opened an opportunity for in CRM.

- If the end of the first year has come and there are still opportunities that are open under the new logo sellers' name in CRM, the new logo and install base sellers will work in good faith to determine if they should be treated as an exception/continue to be "held" in the new logo seller's name, or if they should transfer to the install-base team.

- In most instances, any "hold" should last no longer than 90 days, after which some sort of commission split or entire transfer to the install base team takes place.

- When a customer has canceled their contract, the install base team gets one full year to attempt to "win back" the business.

- If a year and a day have passed without a win-back, the account becomes a fresh prospect for the new logo team to pursue again.

In recent years, there has also been a trend to create a third role—the renewals team—that reports to sales operations or finance. Organizations structured in this way have often looked at the gross retention numbers we discussed in Chapter 1 and noted that they have an install base of generally happy customers who have very high renewal rates. If over 95% of your customers are going to renew without needing to be persuaded, it doesn't make a lot of sense to spend a seller's time processing this paperwork or to pay them a commission when they do so.

The renewals team, then, is a lower-paid, more administrative role that communicates with customers about their upcoming renewals and sends invoices that include the maximum price increase the contract allows. Rather than earning commission on every renewal contract, they generally earn an MBO for achieving a gross retention target in these accounts.

Many CROs have a visceral, negative reaction to this setup when they first encounter it. Their title is "Chief Revenue Officer," they argue, so it would only make sense that every revenue-generating activity falls somewhere inside their organization. However, when they see it in practice, they find that their company benefits from this approach by setting up a dynamic where the customer can't trade off price increases for additional product sales. Organizations that make renewals part of the install-base seller's job may be tempted to offer an incentive of "no price increase this year" or "less price increase this year" if the module is purchased at the time of renewal.

When the roles are separated, you've created a dynamic where customers who request relief on price increase in exchange for new product purchases are honestly told by the seller, "I'm sorry, I don't have control over that part of your relationship with us," and the renewals team can say, "Whether you buy a new product or not, my job is just to administrate your current contract, which specifies that this is the increase due." It's not a frictionless customer experience, and in practice, the sales and renewals team will collaborate and make exceptions a number of times. But this structure maximizes the total spend available from the install base and costs the least amount of commission, which maximizes the return your PE investor will make from owning your company.

There are also cultural benefits in separating install base sales from account renewals. Simply stated, writing commission plans for install base teams who are responsible for renewing and growing their accounts is hard to get right. I've seen a lot of organizations blend the two goals, giving sellers a book of business they're tasked with growing 20% through renewal and upselling, paying a flat commission rate on every dollar sold. In practice, this plan under-rewards the things that sellers spend most of their efforts on—introducing new products to customers—and penalizes them for things they often can't control.

Consider two sellers, each with a $2M book of existing business that they're tasked with growing to $2.4M. They each have a $100k variable target, so earn 4.16% on every dollar sold. One seller—we'll call him "Lazy Larry"—doesn't spend any time introducing new products to his clients, but benefits when 97% of his customers renew their contracts. He earns a little over $80k through his commission plan, though he did very little work.

Another seller—we'll call her "Unlucky Ursula"—works hard to sell $400k of new products into her accounts. But when her biggest client, who spends $500k annually with her company, goes bankrupt, her gains in the territory are completely wiped out. She worked much harder than Larry all year long but earned $1,667 less than he did under the same commission plan.

Lazy Larry	Unlucky Ursula
• $2M book of business • $400k growth target • $2.4M quota • 100k variable • 4.16% commission on all dollars sold • 97% of customer renew effortlessly • Sells no new products	• $2M book of business • $400k growth target • $2.4M quota • 100k variable • 4.16% commission on all dollars sold • 500k customer goes bankrupt • Sells 400k of new products
$1.94M attainment $80,833 commission	$1.90M attainment $79,166 commission earned

Fig 2.1 A Tale of Two Install Base Sellers

Some organizations try to account for this by splitting their variable pay into two components, the upsell/expansion and the renewal, and then assigning different commission rates for each of them. However, it's hard to find a split that results in commission rates that will meaningfully influence behavior. Figure 2.2 shows a plan that assigns 20% of the seller's variable pay to the renewal and 80% to upsell activity. The resulting 1.053% commission rate is so small, however, that losing a $500k renewal would impact their overall variable earnings by just over 5%, and barely over 2.5% of their total earnings if their base salary and variable are the same.

The impact on total pay is so negligible the seller is unlikely to do much to try to rescue these at-risk accounts (if that's even possible). There are just too few dollars at play to garner their attention, and that's on a large account that comprises 25% of their book of business. The dollar amounts are even smaller and less impactful on renewals for smaller accounts. Losing a $100k renewal affects the seller's compensation by $1,052 before taxes. In this scenario, I'd argue that the effort of administering this plan isn't worth the small variation in pay it creates and would simply make "working to renew the book of business" an expectation that the seller's base pay compensates.

$2M Book of Business 95% Renewal Target 20% Expansion Target $100k Variable Pay		Renewal	Upsell
20/80 Plan	Variable	$ 20,000	$ 80,000
	Commission Rate	1.053%	20.000%
50/50 Plan	Variable	$ 50,000	$ 50,000
	Commission Rate	2.632%	12.500%

Fig 2.2 Two Comp Plans that Attempt to Reward Renewal and Upsell

Figure 2.2 also shows a 50/50 plan that attempts to correct for this issue of "too few dollars at play to matter to the seller" by nearly doubling the commission earned for renewal dollars. Yet it does so at the expense of drastically reducing the commission rate for upsell—from 20% to 12.5%—which seriously devalues the effort and importance of being in front of customers to pitch new products. Seeing this play out in multiple organizations, I've come to believe that we're best served when our install base sellers focus exclusively on expansion and growth activities and an operations or finance team manages the renewals - earning, perhaps, a $5k MBO each quarter for maintaining a net retention target.

Separating Segments

Once you've separated the new logo sales team from the install base sellers, it's helpful to segment sub-teams by the size of prospect they pursue. The largest enterprise-sized customers have the most complicated sales, which may involve managing relationships with more than a dozen decision-makers at the account. These should be worked by your most senior, most skilled sellers. A more junior "Midmarket" sales team can be deployed to the smaller, easier-to-navigate prospects, and an entry-level inside/telesales team can handle Small/Medium Business (SMB) accounts who may largely engage in self-service purchases driven by automated emails, videos, and marketing nurture sequences.

Having these three sales segments gives you an opportunity to offer a nice career progression for your sellers. Millennial employees generally want to be promoted every six to twelve months, but may not yet have the skill to move from one selling team to another. Rather than letting them jump ship for another company to chase a small increase in pay, you can set up progressions from SMB to Senior SMB roles, or Midmarket Level 1, 2, and 3 with small shifts in compensation and quota to fulfill this need. You can then offer larger promotions from the SMB to the Midmarket team or from Midmarket to Enterprise over the multi-year timeframe it may take your sellers to develop the necessary skills to succeed in more complex accounts. By doing so, you can incrementally extend a seller's tenure within your organization, which has major impacts on the ramped "quota on the street" you modeled in your annual plan.

Assigning Territories Within Teams

At this point, you've created new logo and install base sales divisions, with smaller teams for their Enterprise, Midmarket, and SMB sellers. Within each of those teams, the next step is to assign a specific territory. In my career, I've met a few sales leaders, particularly at smaller, founder-led companies, who encourage a free-for-all, "first one in the door gets the account" approach to territory allocation.

There are a few reasons why this doesn't work for sales teams of any size:

- It's inefficient to coordinate. New leads often take a while to develop. For many enterprise software companies, it may take as many as 17 touches to generate a first sales meeting with a new prospect. That is often a combination of marketing activity, emailing, calling, and more. When multiple people are trying to "get in the door first," your company risks having a disjointed approach to these first group of touches and is bound to have disagreement on whose effort generated the meeting when it actually lands.

- Best practices don't get shared. When you've got multiple sellers competing against one another, they're less likely to share their best tips and tricks with each other. As a sales leader, you want to identify the best, most effective, and efficient messages for lead generation and get them in use as widely as possible. Giving your sellers their own protected territories removes any disincentive for sharing materials between sellers.

- Inbound leads are hard to assign. While much of your opportunity will be generated by outbound effort, you will still have people come to your website and request a sales call because they found you online or were referred by someone else. Without assigned territories, there's no great way to assign these out. "Round Robin" turn-taking is one approach I've seen implemented, but it leads to complaints that "all the good ones" or "all the largest ones always go to someone other than me." Having pre-assigned territories avoids this problem entirely.

When I create territories, I aim to do so in a way that gives each seller an equal opportunity to succeed, at least across those with the same title on the same segmented team. Some sales leaders have disagreed with me on this approach, saying that they want to give the most lucrative patches to their best sellers. I'd argue that you've already done this when you've put your best sellers in your enterprise teams. Within the team, though, you'll want to ensure that each seller has an equal opportunity to succeed, with equal patches and earning potential. When we assign territories fairly, we've eliminated as much variation as possible from our teams' potential for success. The "best sellers" rise to the top because they truly have the best skills, not because they happened to have more opportunity given to them.

Middle-of-the-pack or worse sellers are quick to find reasons to explain their lackluster performance, and saying that the best seller had an unfair advantage is an excuse that is easy to latch on to. You'll do great things for morale if you ensure there's an even playing field at the start of the year. When you eventually fire a low-performing seller, you'll also have taken away their argument that they were set up to fail with a worse territory than their better-performing peers.

Creating Fair Territories

To create individual territories, you'll want to start with what I call the "Universe List." Using whatever source you have available, try to create a list of every organization that exists in your Total Addressable Market. An Excel spreadsheet with their name, headquarters address, and industry classification is a great place to start—plus any additional information you might know about them. Potential revenue or user counts are great if you have them, but you can use their reported annual revenues and employee counts as a meaningful substitute. You certainly know if they're already a customer, and you can segment these out to an account management team. Perhaps you also have data on whether they're using a competing solution and who it is.

Maintaining the Universe List is an ongoing process. I like to refresh it at least every six months and have had great success outsourcing to low-cost, overseas call centers to conduct basic surveys to fill in missing data. It's also a great project for college interns who get great results when calling with a message like, "I'm a student at the University of Illinois who is learning about your industry as part of my summer internship. Can you help me by answering three quick questions about technologies your business uses to address XYZ problems?"

With these data in hand, you can start experimenting with different territory assignments to see how well-balanced they are across a number of dimensions, including a mix of large and small accounts, greenfield vs. competitive takeaway opportunities, and total revenue potential. You're probably not going to get perfectly balanced territories on all these dimensions, but you can use your best efforts to balance the most important ones for your situation.

Choosing Territory Groupings

Whenever possible, I'm a fan of creating territories based on geography. Certainly, at the world, regional, or country level, language is a first place to start grouping territories. While the post-COVID selling environment includes more web-based selling than ever before, teams still get a lot of success from being face-to-face with their prospects. Creating geographic territories makes the most efficient use of your sellers' time - whether you have enough sellers to make territories that are groupings of major European cities, US states, or just postal codes within them.

I've seen organizations create territories by dividing accounts by letter of the alphabet. I cringe every time I see this. Even if you can avoid disagreement about what a company's "real name" (and thus alphabet letter) is, these distinctions may cause two sellers to buy plane tickets to visit two companies in the same building, when a geographic territory would have saved this duplicate cost. Geographic territories also allow sellers to plan activities across a city, using messages like, "I'm already in town to visit another customer and would love to meet you while I'm there," which also makes them more efficient.

Within a geographical area, you should assign accounts to a territory based on the address of their headquarters location. Let your sellers manage the entire account as one, rather than having different subsidiaries being managed by different sellers, even if the subsidiary is capable of making an independent purchase decision. When the same seller covers all of the divisions and subsidiaries, they're more likely to have important relationships and know important details about internal politics that will help your customers leverage synergies they may not even be aware of.

Deciding which state, city, or postal code belongs in which territory is a bit more art than science, and you'll find there are a few good alternatives for your final territory map. As you start adding and removing cities or states to a territory to balance them out, pay particular attention to key airports and the markets they serve, too. As a Chicagoan, I know it's a great hub city to fly to most places in the Midwest, but my experience is that there's only one flight a day on my preferred airline that goes to Denver, making an "out and back on the same day" sales call pretty difficult to manage. Similarly, you'll find pockets of the country where it's just easier to get to from a certain list of other places, so plan accordingly.

Even for teams in completely virtual, selling-from-home environments, geographic territories are helpful for network building and referral selling. Key decision-makers move around from company to company within their local city, and generally have a network of business contacts, friends, and neighbors there, too. When a seller has a relationship with a good client, a geographic territory allows them to continue selling to them when their key contact goes somewhere else. It also allows the seller to mine referrals from their contacts who don't change jobs.

Occasionally, I've seen organizations divide their sales teams by the industry they serve. I tend to avoid this unless I've got a product that is so industry-specific that the skills required to sell it into one type of account don't translate to prospects in a different segment. While industry specialization may be beneficial when things are going well, small market changes can tank the performance of the entire team simultaneously when they're not.

During the COVID pandemic, any seller whose territory was exclusively made up of restaurants and bars was hard-pressed to find a prospect who was even open, let alone willing to spend money on new solutions. Even in less extreme times, there are industry-specific trends like the price of gas or the passing of key pieces of legislation that can wipe out opportunity in an entire industry for a period of time. By giving your sellers accounts in a variety of industries, you ensure they have other places they can devote their time and energy to when things drop off in one, much in the way you'd balance a stock portfolio.

Balancing territories takes a bit of trial and error to get right, and I tend to use Excel plus some pivot tables to put different postal codes or states in and out of a territory to see the effect it has on overall balance. There are also a number of software packages that can be used to overlay data onto geographic maps to make things easier. Regardless of the tool, it should be possible to narrow in on some pretty good, fairly balanced territories after three or four iterations of experimentation.

Communicating Territory Assignments

Once you've set your territories, your last step is to roll them out with a good communication plan. Be sure that each quota carrier receives a written document that describes their territory and the other details of their compensation plan. It's best practice to have them sign to acknowledge receipt and return to you as well. When you send the document out, your email message might provide some background information on how you arrived at the territories, the things you were balancing for, and other statements that will build confidence in your sellers that they each have the ability to succeed.

In the document itself, spell out your transition plan from any current territory assignments to the new one. Include the date these territories take effect. Also, include a "hold policy" for deals that sellers are currently working in their "old" territory.

My policy generally says:

- The seller needs to register a list of deals they want to hold today.

- I reserve the right to reject their requests and expect that it will be a very short list, regardless.

- The seller has 90 days to close deals on their hold list before they get reassigned to a new seller.

- If we generally agree that a deal is making forward progress but is taking a very long time, we'll start to introduce the new seller and create a step-down process for "splitting" revenue (the sooner it closes, the more quota the original seller retires).

As with all compensation plans, I also include language that reserves the right for the leadership team to make changes or exceptions at their discretion at any point in time, though hopefully, we've built something sensible enough that I won't need to use that authority often. Assigned territory is one of the key factors that influence a quota carrier's satisfaction with their job, and changes to them can have a big impact on short-term morale. That's why I try not to change territories very often. Ideally, just one time in my tenure as CRO under a given PE owner. Territory changes are best communicated at the same time as compensation plan changes, and as we'll see in Chapter 4, those should happen on the first day of a new fiscal year.

CHAPTER 3

SMarketing Collaboration

I first heard the word "SMarketing" in 2016. I was interviewing for a role as a country CEO with a focus on rejuvenating the sales organization, and I was surprised to see that the BDR team was reporting up to the CMO, rather than the VP of Sales.

That was completely different than any of my previous experiences, and I had a long conversation with the CMO about whether that was open for negotiation. She graciously explained to me that the reporting relationships didn't really matter as long as everyone was aligned on what we were trying to achieve and how we would all get there together, describing this as a "SMarketing culture."

I was over a decade late to this party.

HubSpot coined the term "SMarketing" in the early 2000s, defining it as the integration of sales and marketing strategies and using constant communication to align the sales and marketing teams, processes, and goals.

As a sales leader, assigning quotas and territories to sellers based on the annual plan is part of making sure that your company reaches its financial objectives. But sellers are just one piece of the puzzle. Their quota achievement is underpinned by the work of marketers, SEO and inbound lead specialists, outbound-calling BDRs, and more. To ensure your success, every one of these players also needs to be in sync with one another, no matter who they report to.

In my career, there have been times that I've managed the full portfolio of Marketing and Sales functions under a single "CRO" umbrella, and I've served as a standalone head of marketing, too. I learned quickly that marketing encompasses several disciplines that most sales leaders don't have expertise in, including brand definition, web design, video production, PR, event management, and more. It's a tough job that everyone thinks they know something about, and marketers are driven crazy by sellers or others who have a strong opinion or suggestion about the color of the company logo, or why they should purchase season tickets to entertain at the Knicks game instead of some other event spend. If you don't have experience with all of those other disciplines, you will probably be a CRO who is a peer to a CMO rather than one who owns all of the teams yourself, and you will likely have some times that the BDR team reports to you and other times that it doesn't.

While I personally like to manage a team that has a head of marketing, a head of BDRs, and a head of sales all reporting to me as co-equals, my 2016 experience taught me that the most important thing is to get those three functions operating with a shared vision, a shared understanding of who is responsible for what, and a commitment to win or lose together, regardless of reporting structures.

It's a hard thing to get right.

I've seen organizations where each month, the CMO celebrated another record-breaking number of marketing-qualified leads sent to the sales organization, which had rejected all of them as "not a fit." I've seen organizations where the CRO demands a higher volume of discovery calls from their marketing and BDR peers, who rightfully point out that they've sent over more than enough opportunities that advance to late stages in the sales cycle, but which the sales organization consistently seems to lose during the final negotiation phase of their process.

It's an age-old story. Sellers from any organization will immediately find common ground with peers at other organizations by complaining that marketing doesn't create enough quality pipeline for them to work on, and marketers complain in equal amounts with peers that they create great leads that poor sellers squander.

Regardless of the volume of leads, egos can create more petty battles about whether a specific lead was marketing-generated or sales-generated, and if it was an inbound opportunity or an outbound one. BDRs are often caught in the middle of these fiercely-fought battles, desperately hoping that they'll get their own slice of attribution credit to earn their own variable compensation goals. At the end of the day, a SMarketing culture sidesteps these questions by creating a unified incentive plan that just generates the leads the company needs to achieve its goal.

It's a lot of work to generate a lead. Most sellers and BDRs tend to make two or three unanswered phone calls and give up when their voice messages go unreturned. That's not nearly enough activity.

It takes a lot of contacts to turn a cold prospect into a warm opportunity. Sources vary in exactly how many is "a lot," but I've heard professionals estimate it as anywhere between 11 and 50 touches. For B2B SaaS sales, I've seen firsthand that it includes tons of emails from people with marketing, BDR, and selling titles. It takes several phone calls from many of those same people, who also send multiple connection requests to prospects on LinkedIn. It takes a great deal of activity in a marketing team that purchases search keywords and banner ads, sets up Account-Based Marketing microsites, and many other complex strategies.

When one of these tactics ultimately results in one of those people filling out a demo request form on the website, it may technically be called an inbound lead, but categorizing the lead as one created because of the SEO work on the website, or because of the final email that contained the link with the call to action, misses the impact that all of the rest of the effort had on getting this opportunity started.

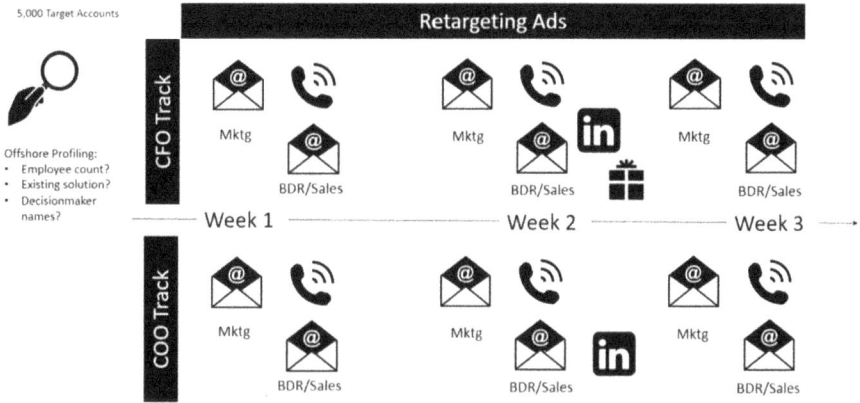

Fig 3.1: Lead Generation Requires Coordination from Multiple People Acting in Sync

While there is some benefit to be had from measuring the dollars spent on a particular messaging campaign or gifting program and comparing it to the revenue generated, the most important issue for me is to make sure that every member of the SMarketing organization understands how they contribute to the goal and are doing their part to advance it.

When it's working well, the results can be phenomenal.

In 2014, I was leading sales for a retail scheduling tech company that had great success in the UK but was just establishing its presence in the US. Our media team had identified a New York Times story about the life of a worker in a chain coffee shop, and I wrote a short LinkedIn article about how her experience could have been different if she had been scheduled with our software. The marketing team made sure my article was getting seen on social media, and my sellers commented and shared the article, too. Soon, I got a call inviting me to come to California to talk about a "Smart Scheduling" ordinance that the city of San Francisco was about to pass. I attended the event, and our marketing team wrote about it. Our BDR team started calling and emailing prospects about the implications it would have for retailers with stores in California.

I blogged a bit more. More social buzz built. Soon, I got a call from the White House inviting me to participate in a task force regarding a potential Retail Workers Bill of Rights, a national law modeled after the San Francisco ordinance. I joined the task force, alongside representatives of name-brand retailers, who my sales team later followed up with. By the end of the year, we'd signed a few dozen new clients as a direct result of all of these activities. It was a great sales result, which came at very little cost.

It's because of experiences like these that I like to track the efforts of SMarketers as a collective whole, rather than as discrete entities. Sure, we work to make each individual component efficient, but I place much more emphasis on understanding the bigger picture of what our combined efforts are creating. Variable compensation plans will provide individual-level incentives and rewards to individual components of the SMarketing engine, but constantly putting those metrics in the larger context of what we're trying to accomplish as a company helps each team member to adjust their ultimate goal when they see the bigger company picture.

To help individual SMarketers understand the even bigger picture, we regularly look at a "Win Creation Waterfall," which aligns us on how many leads are necessary to achieve the annual plan. The waterfall works backward from the total revenue goal we're chasing, using historical win rates and deal sizes to determine just how many opportunities our sellers need to be engaging to get the result we're looking for. Further upstream, show and conversion rates from each of our lead generation channels can tell a BDR or an SEO specialist exactly how much of their activity will be needed to support the overall plan:

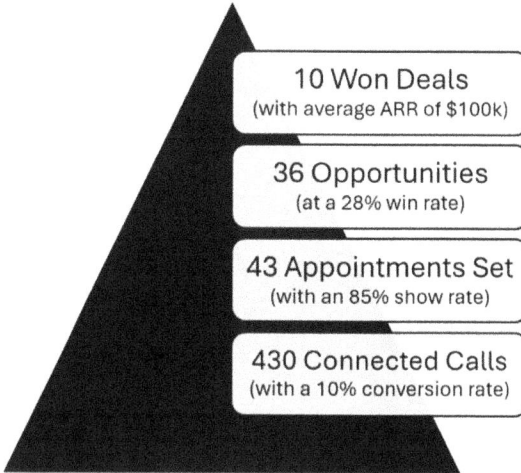

Fig 3.2: A Win Creation Waterfall Shows the Metrics that Lead to $1M of Booked Sales

Length of average sales cycle by team also interacts with win rates and the annual plan to inform how much pipeline is needed each month to achieve success in subsequent months. Figure 3.3 shows, for example, a new logo team with a 32% win rate and a six-month sales cycle will need to have created $2.1M of pipeline in June if they expect to close $700k of revenue by December, while an install-base team that wins 80% of their opportunities with a two-month sales cycle may only need to have $320k of pipeline created in January to close more than a quarter million dollars of business in March.

Your specifics will vary. While we ultimately want to recognize the success of teams that achieve or beat a particular metric (for example, celebrating when a digital marketer achieves a particular conversion rate), the business doesn't succeed unless that metric interacts with all the rest to produce the ultimate revenue goal.

In 000's
Bookings By Team By Month

	JAN	FEB	MAR	APR	MAY	JUN	JUL	AUG	SEPT	OCT	NOV	DEC	TOTAL
Sr. New Logo	0.15552	0.23328	0.3888	0.171072	0.256608	0.42768	0.171072	0.256608	0.42768	0.279936	0.419904	0.699984	3.888
Jr New Logo	0.0864	0.1296	0.216	0.09504	0.14256	0.2376	0.09504	0.14256	0.2376	0.15552	0.23328	0.3888	2.16
Install Base	0.10368	0.15552	0.2592	0.114048	0.171072	0.28512	0.114048	0.171072	0.28512	0.186624	0.279936	0.46656	2.592
Renewal	1.3824	2.0736	3.456	1.52064	2.28096	3.8016	1.52064	2.28096	3.8016	2.48832	3.73248	6.2208	34.56
Total	1.728	2.592	4.32	1.9008	2.8512	4.752	1.9008	2.8512	4.752	3.1104	4.6656	7.776	43.2

In 000's
Pipeline Needed By Team By Month

	JAN	FEB	MAR	APR	MAY	JUN	JUL	AUG	SEPT	OCT	NOV	DEC	TOTAL
Sr. New Logo	0.5346	0.8019	1.3365	0.8748	1.3122	2.187	12.15						19.197
Jr. New Logo	0.3277241	0.4915862	0.8193103	0.3277241	0.4915862	0.8193103	0.5362759	0.8044138	1.3406897	7.4482759			13.406897
Install Base	0.324	0.14256	0.21384	0.3564	0.14256	0.21384	0.3564	0.23328	0.34992	0.5832	3.24		6.156
Total	1.1863241	1.4360462	2.3696503	1.5589241	1.9463462	3.2201503	13.042676	1.0376938	1.6906097	8.0314759	3.24		38.759897

Fig 3.3: Month-by-Month Pipeline Generation Requirements by Team

The annual plan isn't complete, then, when it just includes bookings targets. It also needs to include targets for each of the leading indicators across the SMarketing organization, including the emails sent and open rates, the calls set and show rates, and everything else that drives a prospect through the Win Creation Waterfall.

When we've got a well-instrumented team tracking each of these items, we'll also find that the formula for success won't stay constant for many months in a row. Things change—for good and for bad—for all sorts of reasons, making one part of the engine overperform and another underperform against prior results.

That's why I calculate "Sales Velocity" on a monthly basis, and share it across all members of the SMarketing team. It uses opportunity count, opportunity size, win rate, and length of sales cycle to calculate a measure of "revenue booked per day." When we're not achieving our target sales velocity, it helps us have an informed discussion about which metrics we can most easily influence, and what that means for the revised performance targets of each team member to help us all succeed.

$$\frac{\#_{\text{Opportunity Count}} \times \$_{\text{Opportunity Size}} \times \%_{\text{Win Rate}}}{L_{\text{Length of Sales Cyle (in days)}}} = V_{\text{Sales Velocity}}$$

Fig 3.4: Calculating Sales Velocity

One of my most frustrating professional experiences was working in an organization that looked only at booked revenue to determine if the sales and marketing teams were "succeeding." Our sellers actually had a healthy win rate of about 32%, and deals closed on a fairly-quick two-month cycle. The total number of opportunities created seemed like a reasonable volume for the number of BDRs and marketers involved, but layoffs in one of our target markets meant that new clients were buying fewer licenses for a much smaller employee base than they had in the past. Similarly, we saw fewer customers proactively calling to expand their contracts to support larger teams, and when they did, the number of new licenses they needed to add was smaller than in previous years.

Our leadership team had endless conversations about why the total revenue produced each month was smaller than our plan called for. My well-intentioned CEO asked if I needed to trade out my sales team for better sellers or implement a new sales training program to win more. Both suggestions were misguided. To reach the performance target we were chasing, we'd have had to double our win rate to something like 70% of all early-stage opportunities.

The CMO was similarly being hounded to double the number of opportunities that entered the pipeline while maintaining their already world-class cost-per-lead spend ratio. Starting from an assumption that no additional dollars could be added to the marketing budget, this strategic suggestion was also a non-starter. Finally, we walked our executive team and board through a discussion on each of the components of our sales velocity metric, comparing each piece to what they'd been in prior years.

Everyone had a breakthrough in understanding. It was deal size that most needed fixing, not sales OR marketing skills. While it didn't happen overnight, we focused our energies on campaigns to a segment of the market that was bigger than we had done previously, and our performance returned to being "on plan" even as the conversion rates of marketing qualified opportunities and win rates of individual sellers stayed largely the same. An organization that has not embraced a "SMarketing orientation" might have spent several cycles pointing fingers at one another—defending their own actions, shifting the blame to someone else, and never getting at the underlying challenges of the business.

By aligning everyone to all of the inputs that lead to revenue success, this team landed in a much more productive place. We course-corrected in ways to achieve our numbers, which achieved our investor's plan. Everyone benefitted. It was a great result. At the end of the day, booked revenue was the ultimate measure of success - but the inputs leading to that success were all SMarketing.

CHAPTER 4
Writing Compensation Plans

The first commission check I ever received was for $14k. I'd been a solutions engineer for three weeks and was just getting trusted to demo the software on my own when the direct deposit hit my bank account, alongside a little over $2.5k for my base pay.

I re-checked my employment agreement and incentive plan before approaching my manager, who said they hadn't made a mistake. As a small startup company with only three SEs, they'd built a plan that paid all of us on every deal sold across the company—regardless of our personal involvement—to encourage us to collaborate with anyone, anywhere, on getting deals done.

A seller in California had closed the largest deal in the company's history shortly after I was hired, creating this surprise windfall for me. My manager told me I'd more than earn it in efforts on future deals, and should just focus on being a good team player, pitching in wherever I could. If that's the outcome they were looking for, they got it. Today, I've flown over a million miles on American Airlines, and stayed almost three whole years in Marriott hotels, with a large portion of that travel accumulated during my earliest selling years under this commission plan.

When I later became a quota-carrying seller with a territory of my own, I received a different incentive plan. Reading it carefully taught me all the ways to maximize my earnings—by bundling certain products together in each of my deals, by never negotiating some contract terms out of the agreement, and so on—and I earned large checks when I followed those rules. Again, my company was driving my behavior by setting the rules through which I'd get paid.

As the name suggests, the sales incentive plan is more than just a document that describes how your sellers will be paid; it is a clear articulation of the kinds of behaviors that you want them to perform and incentivizes them accordingly. The best sellers look at their incentive plan as a set of rules in a game they intend to beat, and immediately find all of the unique loopholes and tricks to maximize the end score, their compensation. That's why a well-written plan can be a powerful tool for attracting and retaining high-performing talent.

Achieving the Right Target Spend

Against a private equity backdrop, your sales incentive plans also need to fit into the overall financial structure of the business. When evaluating businesses, a lot of investors look to a calculation of their "Sales Magic Number" or "Customer Acquisition Costs (CAC)." Those are slightly different measures of sales efficiency that look at the total spend it took to generate one dollar of ARR. Because it costs very little to renew an existing customer, many organizations are comfortable spending a bit more than a dollar to secure a dollar of recurring revenue—including all sales and marketing costs involved in securing that win—because the cost of renewing that dollar in following years will be very low.

In new logo sales, one of the biggest drivers of sales cost is the compensation of the seller, and a good rule of thumb is that their annual ARR quota should be between three and five times their on-target earnings. For example, a seller whose target compensation is $250k should have a quota of between $750k and $1.25M of ARR to be sold. When we've built compensation plans this way, we're almost guaranteed to maintain an appropriate cost of sale for top-performing sellers, low-performing sellers, and everyone in between.

Incentive Plan Components

There are many kinds of sales jobs that come with a variety of compensation structures. The standard for B2B tech sales, however, offers sellers a mix of guaranteed base pay along with a variable component. These are generally planned in a 50/50 ratio, so our seller with $250k in On Target Earnings (OTE) will earn $125k of base pay, and a commission plan that pays out another $125k if they achieve 100% of their quota.

The guaranteed base recognizes that selling complex software is hard. It takes a long time to land deals that will ultimately be high-value to the company, and the base pay helps smooth out the earnings for sellers as they invest the up-front time in building relationships. The base pay is also compensation for all of the "table-stakes work" involved in the job—keeping CRM reports updated, attending training, and doing all the other things we ask of sellers that aren't directly tied to closing business.

The variable component of their compensation is pay for performance. The more a seller sells, the more money they earn. Sales recruiters often tout that a given company offers "uncapped commission," meaning that the potential earnings are limitless. In practice, this should be an unnecessary qualifier. No organization should cap commissions to their sellers. It's demotivating to sellers after they've achieved their quota, and a well-written plan should continue to be profitable to the company as they continue to sell past that goal. While not strictly part of "compensation," the incentive plan should also stipulate that sellers will be fully reimbursed for expenses they incur as part of their job, including costs of driving a personal vehicle to visit prospects, hotel, airfare, and meals when traveling overnight, and client entertainment expenses.

I once worked with a CEO who suggested that we should track expenses against each prospect, and only reimburse the seller if they win the deal in the misguided belief that it would increase win rates. Not only would that have had an extremely negative impact on culture, but it's potentially illegal in states like California, whose labor code 2802 also requires reimbursement of all necessary expenses reasonably incurred in the course of their employment, including cellphone bills and a host of other items. The CEO looking to control sales expenses would be better served by writing a clear reimbursement policy that lays out guidelines for the kinds of expenses that are appropriate (which class of airline service to use, types of entertainment that are/are not acceptable for clients) along with a spending threshold that might require pre-approval before committing to it.

Base Salary

The base salary is perhaps the easiest part of an overall seller's compensation plan to administer. It should be about 50% of the seller's OTE. In the US, it is customarily paid every two weeks, while other countries pay this once monthly. Within the same job title, all sellers should have the same base pay to reflect that they have the same job expectations. In practice, the demands of a specific market may require deviation from that standard. Similarly, the market conditions and available talent pool when a specific seller is hired may also cause some small deviations. It's important to work closely with your HR business partner who can develop a "salary band" for each role in your team that allows for such flexibility but doesn't run afoul of providing equal pay for equal work across your employee base.

There are some organizations that have policies that "salespeople never get raises." Their explanation is that sellers have a lot more control over their earnings through variable pay, and so "if you want to make more, you should sell more." It's often difficult to explain these policies to sellers, and demoralizing when they attend all-company meetings and hear that annual review time has resulted in raises for different teams.

If at all possible, I like to encourage my HR teams to give all sellers a standard cost of living adjustment each year, usually 1-3%. This is also a great time to adjust for minor disparities across the team, bringing everyone up to the same standard base pay. In practice, most HR teams I've worked with have actually followed a cycle where those adjustments are reviewed and implemented at least every other year, and there are a handful of mid-year adjustments made for individual sellers with unique special circumstances.

Commission Accelerators

Within the variable component of a seller's pay, there are a number of ways to structure the plan. While the most straightforward approach is to simply divide the variable compensation by the quota to arrive at a commission rate, an accelerated plan that pays higher commissions when more quota is retired has a number of benefits.

For easy math, let's consider a sales team with quotas of $1M of booked ARR and variable compensation of $100k. A linear commission plan would simply pay out 10% on the ARR of all signed deals.

To create an accelerated plan, you might base the first $50k of variable comp on reaching $600k of bookings (an 8.33% commission rate), and the remaining $50k on the next $400k of bookings (a 12.5% commission rate). For bookings over $1M, you might accelerate even further with an equal step up to a 16.6% rate.

For sellers achieving 100% of quota, the earnings are exactly the same under either plan. But look at the impact under a variety of performance scenarios:

Seller	Attainment	Linear Plan	Accelerated Plan
James Patterson	134%	$ 134,000.00	$ 156,440.00
Emily Davis	107%	$ 107,000.00	$ 111,620.00
Michael Brown	98%	$ 98,000.00	$ 97,500.00
Jessica Wilson	92%	$ 92,000.00	$ 90,000.00
David Johnson	87%	$ 87,000.00	$ 83,750.00
Ashley Smith	83%	$ 83,000.00	$ 78,750.00
Christopher Jones	68%	$ 68,000.00	$ 51,000.00
Sarah Williams	54%	$ 54,000.00	$ 45,000.00
Matthew Miller	23%	$ 23,000.00	$ 19,166.67
Amanda Anderson	14%	$ 14,000.00	$ 11,666.67
Total Commissions		*$ 760,000.00*	*$ 744,893.33*

Fig 4.1: Commission Payouts Under Accelerated and Linear Plans

The top seller in this example earns over $22k more under an accelerated plan. Their higher payout is a huge motivation for them to "keep selling" in the current year, vs. letting end-of-year deals slide into the next year to get a head start on that quota. Their higher payout also creates an additional incentive for them to stay at the company.

At the other end of the scale, the bottom performers earn less under the accelerated plan. These are the sellers that you don't want to retain anyway – so the less money you spend on their compensation, the better. Lower earnings may actually accelerate their decision to leave the company voluntarily, which can be helpful to all involved. An added bonus is the accelerated plan serves your goals for the top performers and low performers while costing less money overall. In this example, the top seller receives more than $22k more commission while the company spends $15k less on the total commission program.

Remember, too, that when we built our annual plan in Chapter 1, we structured it in a way that we are succeeding when our sellers are achieving 80% of their quota. Creating an accelerated plan in this way means that we may achieve 100% of the company's planned bookings, but pay significantly less than 80% of our commission budget to get there, assuming we're not hitting the collective target through wild overperformance of just one or two sellers. This cost savings has a positive impact on EBITDA and Rule of 40 attainment and is a great place to look to fund unexpected costs that come up during the year.

Get A Commission Plan Modelling Tool at

bit.ly/3XjIcUD

Occasionally, a CFO worries that these accelerated plans are "too rich" at the top end. They worry about what would happen if a given seller achieves 200%, 300%, or more of their quota. In these instances, my advice is clear: Pay them.

If you've built quotas and balanced territories appropriately, you are unlikely to have a large number of sellers overachieving by such large margins. Performance is more likely to follow a typical bell curve distribution, and the overall program cost associated with paying one seller extremely high commissions is likely to be offset by savings from sellers at the lowest end of the curve.

Moreover, the fact that there is a seller earning over a million dollars in commission is news that will get around among the rest of the team, motivating your low performers to work harder. It also establishes your company as an attractive employer capable of recruiting top talent from outside the organization, too.

What if you happen to have a year where many, or even the majority, of your sellers have achieved more than 100% of their goal? This, too, should not be a problem. In our annual plan, we anticipated that we'd achieve our target if only 80% of sellers achieved 80% of plan. A year with very widespread overperformance, means, by definition, that the company is exceeding its overall plan and can easily absorb a less-than-textbook CAC or Sales Magic Number. You'll also adjust quotas the following year to account for this proven ability to perform at a new, higher level.

Creating Other Incentives

Within this general framework, you might further tweak the plan to incentivize important behaviors for your year. In a year where selling multi-year deals is important, sellers might get a slightly lower commission rate for one-year deals than they do for three-year ones. Perhaps you've launched a new product that you want to be sure your sellers familiarize themselves with, and want to give a higher commission rate for sales of those products. Maybe quarter-to-quarter consistency is an important goal, and you want to have accelerated commission rates that reset each quarter, or that allow sellers to "lock in" a higher rate for next-quarter sales by achieving a certain threshold this quarter.

In designing these systems, it's important not to make them too complicated. Sellers do best with easy-to-understand plans that have just one or two variables, and you'll want them to be able to easily calculate their own projected earnings at any given time with a pencil and a small sheet of paper.

At the company level, you may have a hard time projecting exactly what your commission costs will be, as you don't know how evenly-spread your deals will be between top, middle, and low-performers. Remembering that the goal is to get 80% of sellers to achieve 80% of their quota, though, I usually have an expense plan that anticipates paying out 80% of the variable earnings in my sellers' comp plans. My actual experience is that I usually have over-budgeted for commission payments, leaving me some extra unspent dollars at the end of each quarter. I use those to fund one-time competitions the following quarter that reinforces my key focus at that point in time, such as, "If you can sell at least two of the new products, you'll earn a one-time spot bonus of $500, with an additional $500 for each additional product you sell in the quarter."

Compensating Ramping Sellers

For companies whose sellers need a while to come up to speed post-hire (because of long sales cycles, lack of familiarity with the product, or under-developed territories), there is always a question about how to compensate new hires. Some organizations choose to offer a "commission draw" program. Essentially, this advances payment to sellers based on their anticipated future earnings, and are offered as either recoverable (the seller needs to pay them back out of future commission checks, or upon leaving the organization) or non-recoverable (in which case, they are simply an extension to base earnings for some period of time).

I've never had a good experience with draw programs. Employees who fail to perform will choose to leave or are asked to leave involuntarily, but repayment of a recoverable draw becomes a sticking point to making that happen. In most cases, the company agrees to forgo the recovery amount owed, creating a non-recoverable draw program in practice— even if it's not the official, stated policy.

Instead of this messiness, I prefer to create a ramping incentive plan to carry new sellers through their onboarding period. The research in building our annual plan already tells us how many months it takes for a seller to become fully productive. If your team usually requires three quarters before achieving that production rate, you can create adjusted "ramping quotas" for those first three quarters, and pay adjusted commission rates to achieve OTE accordingly.

Alternatively, for teams that expect zero production for a given length of onboarding time, I prefer to reward the behaviors that set the new seller up for success. Here, I offer sellers the ability to earn a monthly or quarterly bonus for achieving the metrics that are your leading indicators of success, whether that be creating the right number of new opportunities in the CRM system, connecting with the right number of new contacts, or advancing the right number of deals through various sales stages on the right timeframes.

Sellers who actually sell products during this ramping period can earn commission for any dollars the commission plan would pay above the guaranteed quarterly bonus through these activities.

Plans for Install-base Sellers

Salespeople responsible for selling to the install base have commission plans very similar to the new logo plans described above, though they tend to have higher quotas and lower OTEs under the belief that it is easier to sell a new product to an existing client than it is to win an entirely new customer.

As I've shared previously, the best practice is for customer renewals to be managed by a separate, non-selling team who generally gets most of their earnings from base pay and a small variable payment tied to renewal success. In these instances, install-base sellers should not have any quota or commission tied to customers who simply renew their existing service according to pre-contracted terms. In smaller organizations, I've seen attempts to have an install-base team manage "a book of customer business" that they are responsible for both renewing and growing. In such cases, a seller may be given a set of accounts who's annual spend is $5M, and told to grow the collective set 20% to $6M by the end of the year.

The problem with this setup is that the loss of a major customer may be outside the control of the seller. If a key client goes out of business, or the product fails in a way that makes them choose not to renew, the seller may find they've got a hole in their book of business that simply can't be filled. With a now-unachievable quota to hit due to a customer loss they had no control over, the best install-base sellers are motivated to leave the company and take jobs where there aren't these perverse incentive plans at play.

Building Plans for Non-Sellers

Many companies have a BDR or SDR team whose responsibilities include setting appointments and qualifying leads for their quota-carrying sellers. These roles, too, should earn variable compensation at a 50/50 base/bonus rate. Yet BDRs can't control the skill of the seller they develop the opportunity for, so it's not fair to tie their earnings to actually seeing their opportunities result in a win. Given the entry-level nature of BDR roles, they may also no longer be in the position when their leads close if the product has a long sales cycle.

Instead, we should look to historic performance and our Win Creation Waterfall to determine how many inputs the BDR needs to put into the system to achieve the company goal. If your sales team has a 33% win rate of opportunities that are set by the BDR, it becomes a simple math problem to calculate how many opportunities they need to create in order to achieve the company's sales goal in their territory to arrive at a "per appointment set" payment rate, again, with accelerating rates when they've achieved 60% and 100% of their target for the month or quarter.

Solutions engineers, who are more closely tied to the success or failure of deals through their demonstration and technical contributions to the sales cycle, tend to have commission plans tied to the quota of the seller(s) they support. Like the organization I first joined as a solutions engineer, some companies may promote team selling and pooling of SE resources by paying their SEs on both the specific deals they are tied to and the performance of the larger team they work for, with a stronger emphasis on their individual contributions. A solutions engineer typically has more base pay than variable pay in their OTE calculations, as do the people who manage BDRs and quota-carriers. Base-to-variable ratios between 60/40 and 70/30 are common for these roles.

Sales "Club" Trips

In the B2B tech industry, it is traditional to offer a "Club" trip to any variable-pay-earning members of the go-to-market team (sales, solutions engineers, BDRs, and managers) who exceed quota, or, perhaps, achieve over 105% of their quota. The trip is an all-expenses-paid vacation for the seller and a guest of their choosing to a destination they'll visit at the same time as other Club achievers.

As I'll discuss in more detail in Chapter 14, social media has made pictures of these trips more visible to non-sales professionals, and some organizations have chosen to expand their Club trips to include top-performing talent from every department to respond to arguments about equity and fairness. Qualification criteria are less straightforward than the numerical quota attainment of sellers, but "achieving the top rating on the annual performance review" or "being in the top 5% of employee performance reviews" are common ways to establish a "Peak Performers Club."

As a CRO, I have no official stake in this debate beyond knowing that my own teams need to have a Club trip. However, I caution organizations that these trips are expected to be high-quality: a nicer vacation than the employee could or would spend their own money on, offering unique experiences they haven't had on their own. Extending this expense to be an "all company" award is no small matter, and once you've broadened the circle of participation one year, it will be next to impossible to reduce it back down to a "sales only" trip in the future.

Communicating the Plan

Once you've carefully designed your incentive plan for the year, you'll want to give just as much attention to crafting the communication of those plans to your team members. The communication is more than just an update about new quotas and commission rates. It's a complete package that lays out to your team the overall company plan, how their piece contributes to it, and what tools are at their disposal to meet—and exceed—the plan. The communication should include examples that easily help sellers calculate their earnings under different achievement scenarios, at 60%, 80%, 100%, and greater attainment.

Whether quotas stayed the same, went up, or (rarely) were lowered, the team should also be shown an achievable blueprint for achieving them. A seller shouldn't just be told that they're expected to sell a million dollars' worth of software. They should be shown their average deal size from the year before, along with the typical sizes of "large" and "small" ones that create a realistic path that, "you will achieve plan if you get three small deals, two average size deals, and one large one." The Win Creation Waterfall is a great illustration to support these communications.

The seller should see that their territory has an appropriate number of prospects to be able to find each of those kinds of opportunities and know that their average sales cycle gives them time to successfully find and close the prescribed number of deals. Sellers should also be shown the typical progression from one sales stage to the next, along with their win rates. If the plan suggests that they need to close six deals a year and they have a 33% win rate, they need to have 18 opportunities in play this year. Working with their BDR or SDR, they should understand the entire Win Creation Waterfall, including how many first appointments need to be set to yield those opportunities. For the BDR specifically, this includes how many outbound calls need to be made to set that many appointments based on prior history.

Marketing colleagues should understand their contributions from inbound lead generation and other channels. Knowing how many days or months it takes to go from cold prospect to closed deal also informs the timing of each of these inputs, including which teams need to do which activities in which month of the year to make it all work together.

Everyone should be aligned on everything that must happen in order to achieve the company's sales objectives. Throughout the year, I regularly check on how actual performance compares to plan. This is not just for the end measure of booked revenue but for measures of each piece leading up to it, too. The best organizations treat their compensation plans as a "contract" with their sellers, requesting that the employee sign off on having received the plan. Your HR and legal teams will have a variety of opinions on whether this is a necessary step.

Almost every well-written plan includes a disclaimer that management "reserves the right to modify the terms at any point in time," though you should strive to never exercise that clause - particularly not when it's a situation of, "We never thought you'd sell that much, and we'd have to pay that much." Some sellers will refuse to sign their plans under the misguided impression that they'll be able to negotiate a better deal if they wait. Don't get drawn into that pointless debate. Simply state in your policy that no commissions will be paid without the signed incentive plan received first. Once the seller's first deal has closed, the situation will resolve itself. These incentive plans and accompanying communications are a lot of material to assemble, and they should all be ready to go, communicated to each individual contributor on the first day of the new year.

If you're ready earlier, you'll want to hold these communications until the current year has finished. You don't want sellers looking at end-of-year deals and trying to game out whether they make more money by closing them this year or next, and you don't want a lot of grumbling about changed territories or comp plans to distract from end-of-year selling.

At the same time, it's not fair to your sellers to withhold this critical information from them after the new year has begun. There are some organizations that just don't seem to be able to get their act together to communicate new territories or quotas until a few weeks or even months into the new year. Sales is a hard job, and every day that goes by without knowing the rules of the game is a lost opportunity. You'll earn a great reputation with your sellers if you can communicate expectations clearly, on time, every year that you work with them.

CHAPTER 5

Talent Assessment, Recruiting, and Management

Most companies I've worked with have an "evergreen" job posting on their website for sales jobs. While these posts receive applications and resumes all year long, there seems to be a particular influx of applicants in the months of November, December, and January.

The timing makes sense to me. As they approach the end of the year, sellers who have had a tough time making their numbers worry that they'll lose their jobs in the new year and start exploring opportunities. Top sellers receive their commission plans for the coming year and make a calculation about whether it's going to be a lucrative one, and after assessing the health of their pipeline decide that they might as well make a change if they're not inspired.

Similarly, I find the start of the year to be an excellent time to decide which of my own sellers I want to continue to bet on in the coming year. By the end of the fourth quarter, I've got an annual plan that gives me a clear view of the company goals for the year and a clear articulation of the expectations I have for each individual to contribute to those goals. And so, it's a perfect time to evaluate whether I have the right talent in the right place to succeed.

I do it by plotting every member of my team on a "Talent Nine Block." McKinsey & Company developed the methodology in the 1970s to help General Electric prioritize investments, and it's been adopted by many organizations in the ensuing decades to evaluate the talent on each of their teams. It is a quick-to-execute assessment that ranks each employee's performance and potential, using a rating scale of solid, high, or low.

Assessing Team Talent

Whenever I join a new organization, I ask my managers to prepare and present the Nine Block to me in the first week. The resulting conversation is a great way for me to get to know something about everyone in the organization, and also a first opportunity for me to assess the talent of my own managers in their ability to assess the quality of their teams in an unbiased manner.

For sales teams, the "Performance" dimension is easy to assess - the manager can look at quota attainment metrics, putting overachievers in the "high" column, sellers who are missing quota substantially in the "low" column, and categorize the rest as "solid." Determining the correct "Potential" row is a bit trickier, requiring the manager to do a qualitative assessment of what the seller is capable of.

Here's what a completed Nine Block might look like for a selling team:

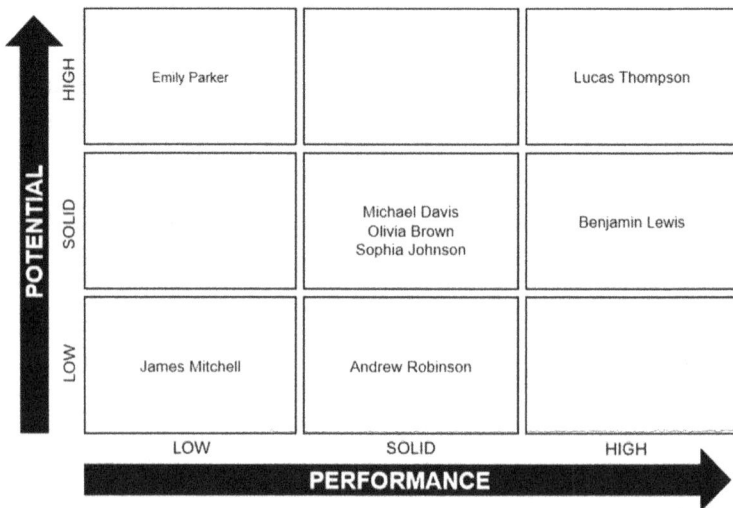

	LOW	SOLID	HIGH
HIGH	Emily Parker		Lucas Thompson
SOLID		Michael Davis / Olivia Brown / Sophia Johnson	Benjamin Lewis
LOW	James Mitchell	Andrew Robinson	

POTENTIAL (vertical axis) / PERFORMANCE (horizontal axis)

Fig 5.1 Charting Team Members by Potential and Performance

Once team members have been placed on the grid, the accompanying Nine Block action grid suggests what their next development action might look like. In a well-performing team, we'd expect the majority of sellers to fit in the middle square: Solid performers with average potential are our middle-of-the-road team members like Michael, Olivia, and Sophia. The clear next step is to see if they can increase their potential over time as a result of our standard training.

Low-potential sellers who nevertheless have performed solidly (like Andrew) are folks that we should continue to work on developing, determining whether coaching can lead to higher performance. Over time, the results should tell us whether they've moved to the right, to the left, or up the center column.

Our new hires should be people we think have very high potential, though ramp time might mean there's no notable performance for a while. This is likely the reason that Emily is placed where she is in the grid – and we should give her some time to settle in and ramp performance, tracking against the typical progress of other new hires. Low performers that we think have very low potential have a clear next step. In this example, James should be managed out of the business or terminated.

Our sellers with high performance and average potential are the strong contributors of the team that we'll count on for reliable results, while the high performers with high potential are the absolute top talent that should be promoted and rewarded to continually-higher levels of responsibility. I'd expect to see Lucas' name on the list of sellers we're considering for promotion in the coming year.

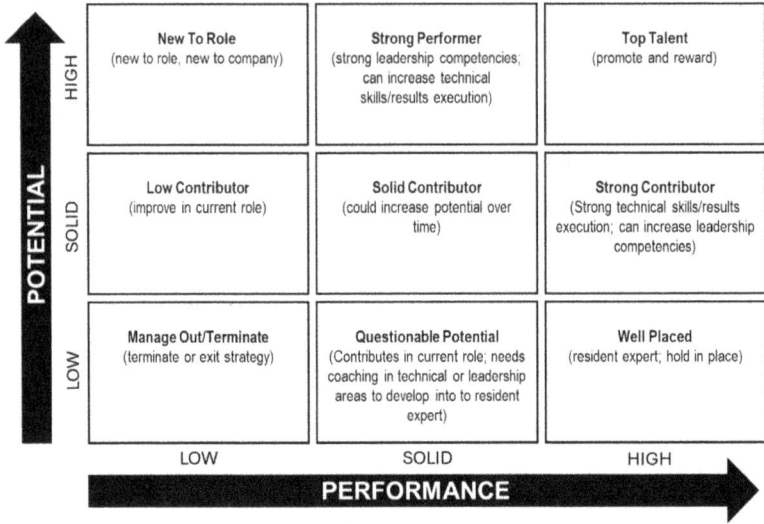

	LOW	SOLID	HIGH
HIGH	New To Role (new to role, new to company)	Strong Performer (strong leadership competencies; can increase technical skills/results execution)	Top Talent (promote and reward)
SOLID	Low Contributor (improve in current role)	Solid Contributor (could increase potential over time)	Strong Contributor (Strong technical skills/results execution; can increase leadership competencies)
LOW	Manage Out/Terminate (terminate or exit strategy)	Questionable Potential (Contributes in current role; needs coaching in technical or leadership areas to develop into to resident expert)	Well Placed (resident expert; hold in place)

POTENTIAL (vertical axis) / PERFORMANCE (horizontal axis)

Fig 5.2 Actions to Take Based on Nine Block Placement

Implement Development Plans

Get a Talent Nine Block Template at

bit.ly/473qKXm

As your managers discuss the Nine Block placements with you, ask them to develop a 90-day plan for each of their sellers based on these guidelines. What skills and abilities does each seller need to work on to move to the next logical level of progression in their role?

Outside of a weekly 1:1 meeting where forecasts and other topics are discussed, managers should have development conversations with each team member at least every 90 days where they make a plan to improve performance. They should begin by agreeing about the quality of the employee's current performance, consider what the next skills progression should be, evaluate current progress against that goal, and create a plan for the next 90 days of development.

Too often, managers and employees view these 90-day "Performance Improvement Plans" as simply an administrative or legal hurdle to document reasons the employee is about to be terminated. That's unfortunate because when performance improvement plans are part of every employee's 90-day cadence, overall performance does, indeed, tend to improve.

Inspect With Managers

On a monthly basis, I like to have a quick check-in with each of my front-line managers to revisit the Talent Nine Block and assess progress. I've had great experience by inviting a sales operations analyst to the meeting who can quickly pull up revenue metrics and quantifiable performance indicators for each team member, alongside an HR business partner who can help with more qualitative measures of success.

Again, the purpose of these monthly reviews isn't necessarily to accelerate the process of exiting anyone from the organization, though they can be effective at doing that when needed, too. Instead, they focus everyone's attention—mine, the manager's, and our business partners'—on what is going on with each individual contributor in the company and what support they need to continue to thrive and perform.

These conversations are particularly enlightening for me, as they give me at least a monthly glimpse into the qualitative, soft issues that don't show up on revenue booking reports. Team members expecting babies, going through home renovations, or dealing with issues related to caring for their elderly parents—all are items that have come up for me in these meetings that I can then take action on or be sympathetic to. The result? Even in teams of up to 200 direct reports, I've been able to make cultural connections like the handwritten sympathy card, or baby gift, or connection to an Employee Assistance Program that helps my sellers feel seen and taken care of – which is great for them and our business.

Develop Succession Plans

As we review Talent Nine Blocks, I also like to ask my front-line managers for their thoughts on succession planning for each role on their team, including themselves. Simply stated, if a role were to become vacant—through the employee's choice, our choice, or some unforeseen circumstance—would we have an internal resource who could step into the role today, or would we need to recruit talent from the outside?

If we have an internal successor or list of successors, likely from the "Top Talent" box of our Nine Block, we write their names into a documented plan. If we don't have an internal successor, we need to think about whose development plan might be able to focus on growing them into it and be sure those relevant skills are being developed.

Recruiting

At this point, you'll want to start working with your HR Business Partner to recruit a replacement for any currently unfilled roles, those filled by low-potential, low performers, or for whom no successor exists.

My recruiting process includes the following steps:

Document Performance Objectives and Key Competencies for The Role

First, I spend time writing down the key performance objectives and competencies for the role. Many of the performance metrics for selling roles are easy to identify. They're the specific things the seller will be held accountable to when they get the job, and the annual plan has already quantified a number of them (quotas, number of calls, and so on).

Key competencies are more qualitative, but they're equally important. They define the specific skills or abilities an individual needs in order to get to the performance metric. Do your sellers need to create the majority of their own pipeline, or will they have a BDR who fills most of their calendar for them? Is the sale an evangelical one that requires the seller to first convince a prospect that a problem exists that needs solving, or is it largely about differentiating your solution from a competitor in a clearly defined category?

When I'm about to start recruiting for a role, I often have several colleagues wanting to introduce me to "the perfect person" in their network that I should hire. But until I can articulate the specific competencies alongside the desired result, I don't want to meet their candidate, because being blinded by a dazzling personality may make me lose sight of the fact that they won't succeed in my specific environment.

It's a lesson I learned through making some hard mistakes. Early in my career, I hired a seller that my manager had worked with in the past. On the objective metrics, their track record was stellar—multiple years of achieving President's Club, an impressive collection of seven-figure deals sold, and brand-name tech companies where he overachieved on quotas that were 50% higher than what they'd be in this job. The manager and I were both excited about having him join the team, and we paid a premium to get this very senior seller into our organization.

Once he was in the role, he started making suggestions and observations, telling me, "The best leads I've ever had were from partners who told their clients they should buy our product." Unfortunately, we didn't have a partner program and it would be years before we'd invest in one. He observed that "It's a lot faster and cheaper to sell a new product to an existing customer than it is to a new one." I agreed, but his role was a new logo one, and there weren't any significant add-on products to sell to the handful of customers we had in this early-stage startup company.

The seller pushed back against suggestions that he spend time making cold calls because, "There's only a 2% response rate from the best email campaigns, and only one in eighty people we call picks up the phone. I'm too senior and get paid too much to spend my day dialing calls that are almost never going to be answered." Yet our lead gen program budgets relied almost exclusively on these labor-intensive, outbound messages from quota carriers.

Hiring this seller after only talking about his objectives did him a disservice. He sold nothing, earned no commission, and wasted six months of his time failing in a job that wasn't suited to him, marring what had previously been a stellar record of multiple years of success. For my company, the opportunity cost from lost time in the territory and the delay in finding and ramping the next seller compounded the financial loss we took by paying more than we wanted to for this senior seller who didn't advance our business. Getting clear on competencies would have given both of us clearer expectations.

My list might have looked like this:

Objective	Competency	Notes
Achieve $1.2M quota	Manage a consultative sales process with the ability to disrupt the customer's thinking.	We sell a complex piece of enterprise software, which involves up to 12 buyers and takes up to 9 months. Our clients are familiar with solutions in this space, but may not know to value our key differentiators.
Close 10 new logo deals a year.	Bring a competitive spirit with proven success as the "underdog."	Our average deal length and size suggest you can, and need to, close 10 deals to hit your quota. While we have a strong solution, we aren't the first name that comes to mind in our category and will usually start from behind in any competitive evaluation.
Develop $3.6M in the pipeline annually, with roughly 30 active opportunities at any one time.	Create a lead generation strategy that is largely executed by you.	With a 30% win rate, you will need approximately 30 opportunities in your pipeline to reach your annual goal. We have a 2:1 coverage ratio of sellers to BDRs. While you will get some support from this team, and our Marketing team has great content for you to leverage, you will need to develop a lot of opportunities on your own.

There may be additional competencies that aren't directly tied to objectives, but which are also table-stakes to success in the role. For example:

Competency	Notes
Dynamic verbal communication and presentation skills, able to connect with a wide variety of individuals.	Our sales process includes multiple decision-makers from various departments and ranges from midlevel managers to c-suite executives. You will need to be adept at engaging with each of them.
Professional written communication skills	We create a lot of written/email communication, formal RFP responses, and proposals in our sales cycles.
Time management and organization	You will have multiple opportunities in play at any one time, involving multiple follow-ups with different stakeholders. You will need to manage them all without missing any of their expectations.
Natural curiosity, intelligence, self-starting problem-solver.	We are a small growing company that does not yet "have it all figured out." We won't be able to tell you exactly what to do to succeed when you walk in the door – we'll be collaborating with you to evolve our messaging, sales plays, and processes through trial and error.

Write the Job Description

With performance objectives and competencies written down, I can now set about writing a job description that will set a candidate's expectations about the details of the role, and get the right folks excited about working in it. Here's what a job description might look like:

Company Overview:

We are a dynamic B2B tech company offering a complex enterprise software solution with unique differentiators. Our clients are typically large organizations with a thorough understanding of the market but may need help realizing the full value of our innovative approach. As a growing company, we value a collaborative, self-starter mentality, and we're looking for someone who thrives in an environment where they can make a significant impact.

Position Summary:

As an Enterprise Sales Executive, you will be responsible for achieving a $1.2M annual quota by closing 10 new logo deals per year. You will manage a consultative sales process, leveraging your ability to disrupt conventional thinking and guide clients toward recognizing the distinct advantages of our solution. You will be adept at developing and executing a lead generation strategy to maintain a pipeline of 30 active opportunities valued at $3.6M annually.

Key Objectives

- Achieve $1.2M annual quota

- Close 10 new logo deals per year

- Develop $3.6M in pipeline annually (30 active opportunities)

Key Competencies

- **Consultative Sales Process:** Demonstrated ability to lead consultative sales processes for complex enterprise software solutions, involving multiple stakeholders and extended sales cycles.

- **Disruptive Thinking:** Ability to challenge customers' assumptions and perspectives, positioning our solution as a superior alternative to established competitors.

- **Competitive Drive:** Proven track record of exceeding sales goals in competitive markets, with a strong ability to position solutions as the "underdog" and win deals against established players.

- **Lead Generation:** Expertise in developing and executing effective lead generation strategies to consistently build a robust pipeline of qualified opportunities.

- **Dynamic Communication:** Exceptional verbal and written communication skills, capable of engaging and influencing a diverse range of stakeholders, from mid-level managers to c-suite executives.

- **Presentation Skills:** Polished presentation skills, able to deliver compelling and informative presentations to both small and large groups.

- **Time Management:** Strong organizational and time management skills, able to manage multiple opportunities simultaneously, prioritize tasks effectively, and meet deadlines consistently.

- **Curiosity and Problem Solving:** Natural curiosity, a proactive approach to problem-solving, and the ability to thrive in a fast-paced, evolving environment where collaboration and creative thinking are essential.

Additional Requirements

- Bachelor's degree in a related field or equivalent experience
- Proven track record of success in B2B software sales
- Experience with enterprise software solutions and long sales cycles

- Strong understanding of the technology landscape and industry trends

Benefits

- Competitive base salary and uncapped commission structure

- Comprehensive benefits package (health, dental, vision, 401k)

- Opportunities for professional development and growth

If you're a highly motivated sales professional with a passion for technology and a drive to succeed, we want to talk with you about this exciting opportunity to join our growing team.

Conduct Interviews

As I interview candidates, I use a very structured approach to assessing each one against every competency. My experience with sellers specifically is that they are likely to be personable folks who can have an entertaining conversation for an extended period of time. It's easy, then, for a seller to go through a poorly-structured interview and have everyone who meets them conclude, "They're a nice person, I enjoyed them, we should hire them." And yet, many sellers hired through that sort of process will be poor fits for the role, because "personability" is only one of many competencies they need to succeed.

To avoid this mistake, I create a grid that scores each of the candidates on 1-5 scale according to their ability to display each of the competencies. I then make sure that each competency is assigned to at least one member of the interview team to probe on and score. Figure 5.3 shows how that might look.

Candidates:	Manage a consultative sales process	Competitive Spirit	Lead generation strategy and execution	Verbal communication skills	Written communication skills	Time Management and Organization	Curiosity/problem solving
Michael Brown				4			1
Janice Cooper							
Jennifer Lee							
Susan Martinez				3			5
David Washingon							

Interview Team:	Scoring Guide:
Robert Johnson	1. Does not demonstrate competency
Patricia Smith	2. Partially demonstrates competency
William Jones	3. Has the competency
	4. Sometimes exceeds competency expectations
	5. Far exceeds competency expectations

Fig 5.3 An Interview Scoring Protocol Grid

Get a Sample Interview Rubric at

bit.ly/3XfFf7g

In this example, Patricia Smith has already completed interviews with Michael Brown and Susan Martinez, testing the verbal communication and problem-solving skills she was assigned to. Patricia determined that Susan had the necessary verbal communication skills and wildly exceeded the expectations for problem-solving, while Michael had better-than-expected verbal communication skills but no problem-solving abilities.

When probing for a skill in an interview, I want my interviewers to ask behavior-based questions. These questions begin, "Tell me about a time when …" and are intended to uncover examples of the candidate actually demonstrating the skill, rather than just reciting an academic answer about how they should behave in a situation.

The interviewer should ask the same questions in the same way across all candidates, and ideally use them every time we're interviewing for this skill and this role. When dozens or hundreds of candidates have been asked the exact same question, it allows the interviewer to really uncover the nuances and fine distinctions between two candidates in a way that can't be uncovered when every interview is conducted differently.

The interviews should also be structured to ensure that every required competency is tested at some point in the cycle. Ultimately the competencies and their associated performance objectives are going to be the things the seller is measured against on a regular basis when they're in the role, and so I want to be sure that I don't make a hire who surprises me with a lack of a skill when they're in the job.

It sounds like a lot of structure, and it is. But it's a process that's been proven to give me the best chance of hiring a candidate who has the best chance of succeeding in the role. And when we consider that our sellers are often the most expensive, most mission-critical hires we make, it's worth the upfront investment of time.

Make A Timely Offer to Your Best Candidate

It's really easy to get into analysis paralysis, continually conducting more interviews in the hopes that someone even better will come along. Recognizing that every day that goes by with a quota-carrying role open means a potential delay in sales, I encourage my managers to make an offer as soon as they have a candidate who meets expectations—scoring 3's on every required competency—even if we have more interviews scheduled with more candidates later on next week. Offers can take a while to get put together, and candidates may take some time thinking about them before ultimately turning them down.

Continuing to bring candidates through the interview process even as an existing offer is out on the street should happen until there is a signed agreement—or possibly even the start date. A surprising number of employees fail to show up for the first day of a new job. Continuing to interview candidates after a role has been filled grows your network, keeps the momentum going in case the preferred candidate drops out for some reason, and gives you a pre-screened candidate to turn to if a similar role becomes available soon.

By the same token, I'm a big fan of ending interviews as soon as I uncover an irredeemable flaw. Once I've determined that a candidate doesn't have a critical competency and I think it would be too expensive or time-consuming to develop it in them, I end the interview. It's a waste of everyone's time—my team's and the candidate's—to continue a slate of interviews that I know will be unsuccessful. If you find yourself in this situation and you're courageous, you should tell the candidate, "We've determined that there isn't a fit for this reason," so they can learn and grow from the experience. However, many folks just end the interview and say there are no more to be scheduled at the moment.

With all of this in mind, I regularly tell my hiring managers that there is no perfect candidate, and that "we hire our own problems." Sellers who are strong in one competency are likely to be weak in another. The managers themselves may be stronger at coaching one skill than they are at another. So, it may also be ok to hire a candidate who doesn't score a 3 on one more of the competencies so long as we're making the hire with full awareness of their deficiency, and believe that we have the skills in place to be able to coach them into competency in a reasonable amount of time.

The CRO's Role In Hiring Skip-Level Employees

Hiring managers often ask me to participate in these interview panels. While I'm happy to play a role, I also make it very clear to the manager (and the candidates) that I am not the ultimate decider, the hiring manager is. Once we hire the seller, that manager is responsible for making sure they perform up to expectations, so that manager needs to decide whether they can overcome whatever shortcomings surfaced in the interview process.

I never want one of my managers to feel that they made a hire because it's the person I wanted, even though they personally had reservations or felt a different candidate would be better. I do tell my managers that I consider my interview a final veto on their decision. I may, on occasion, find a candidate so deficient in some critical way that I refuse to approve the hire. Most often, though, I have a discussion with the manager about where I see potential problems, ensure the manager has a plan to coach them, verify that the manager is confident they can develop the candidate to the acceptable level of performance, and then approve the hire with those plans in mind.

This process means I don't always get my way, and I don't always see my preferred candidates win. I've referred many people into interview processes with the guidance that, "I know this candidate and had a great experience before, but recognize it is not my hire to make." I've regularly seen them passed over for completely different candidates who worked out as well as or better than my own would have. I've strongly felt that some candidates weren't right for whatever reason, but watched the manager hire and coach them to overcome my objections and be top performers. And I've seen managers reject my concerns, only to come back later and say, "You were right, I shouldn't have hired this one."

We'll never get it perfect, but if we're all clear on the objective we're trying to reach, the skills we think are necessary, and the person who is the ultimate arbiter of the decision, we wind up conducting a hiring process we're all happy with, regardless of the ultimate outcome.

A Note On Diversity

When filling quota-carrying roles, we have a lot of urgency to get sellers hired and working the open territories as soon as we can. But we shouldn't let that stop us from conducting a panel of interviews with a number of candidates. How many? It's hard to say, but it's certainly more than one.

In my own processes, I tell my HR partners that I want to see a diverse slate of candidates that represents the makeup of the overall talent pool. For many people, diversity means demographic items like age, race, sex, sexual orientation, disability, and veteran status. Those are certainly the easiest measures to benchmark against, but diversity also might include socioeconomic background, educational background, or some other characteristic that's particularly important to the products you sell. It's an unfortunate fact that when we rely on our social networks to source candidates, we wind up finding a lot of people who look a lot like us in these dimensions. That can create an echo chamber of ideas over time where "nobody who is (fill in the blank) works in (this particular role or field)."

My PhD in organizational communication taught me that diverse groups have been proven over and over to make the best decisions, producing better results for their organizations than homogenous ones do. It makes me particularly interested in hiring diverse teams over time. In practice, that doesn't mean that I'm looking to hire someone from a particular demographic for my next open role. It does mean, though, that I don't consider the interview process over until I've seen a candidate pool that's representative of the overall talent pool out there.

I once joined a small organization that had only male sellers, and none of them were more than 30 years old. My HR partners and I recognized that 25% of the sellers in our target markets were women, and we knew we were going to at least double the size of the team over the course of the next few years. With this in mind, we didn't close any roles until we'd seen a pool that had at least 25% female applicants. Being a woman wasn't a deciding factor in our hiring process. It wasn't even a tiebreaker between candidates. But by forcing ourselves to look beyond just the networks of our existing sellers, who were mostly men in their 20s, we found a lot of talented people who were different from what we already had hired. In a surprisingly short amount of time, my sales team started to look like the rest of the world we operated in.

We had men and women of many different races and ages on our team, and since we were screening for key competencies in each interview, the newly-hired team performed better than the organization had ever seen before.

CHAPTER 6

Sales Playbooks and Methodologies

My experience as an employee of a 26-person company was dramatically different from my experience at the same company when we were 6,000 strong.

A mentor at an even larger organization—who had 6,000 employees in the City of Chicago alone, and hundreds of thousands of employees worldwide—explained that small companies have the luxury of hiring top-tier talent who can thrive independently, figuring out what it takes to succeed. The company's small size also facilitates easy sharing of best practices, enabling continuous improvement.

In contrast, larger organizations face slower communication and challenges with disconnected teams. Finding thousands of exceptional employees becomes difficult, and managers need to shift from a style that empowers their teams with complete autonomy to aligning everyone towards a common goal through the implementation of common processes. As a CRO at a large company—or one with aspirations to be large—a key tool to support this large-scale collaboration is a documented Sales Playbook.

Once a year, I publish a physical Sales Playbook that's updated with everything my teams need to know to succeed. A digital version is integrated into our training and CRM systems to remind sellers of skills at key moments in their sales cycles, and most keep the spiral-bound guide on their desks for quick reference.

The playbook has a few key sections:

Roles and Responsibilities

This section lists every position in our go-to-market organization, along with their responsibilities. For example:

- Commercial Sales Executives are responsible for growing our client base by signing new clients who have up to 500 users.

- Enterprise Sales Executives are responsible for new clients with 501 users and above.

- Account Managers (install base sellers) are assigned a set of customers whose ARR totals $5M and are responsible for growing that book of business 20% through the upsell and expansion of our solutions within those customers. They are not responsible for customer satisfaction (customer success handles that), support (our helpdesk does that), or contract renewals (this is managed by our sales ops organization).

- The Renewals team is part of sales operations and is responsible for ensuring our customers renew their contracts and have price increases applied in accordance with the terms of their contracts.

- Business Development Representatives are responsible for supporting our Sales Executives by creating qualified appointments with an articulated need and one of the other BANT qualification criteria. They are aligned with a Sales Executive in a 1:1 ratio so that every seller is teamed with a BDR, with whom they collaborate to create new opportunities.

- Solutions Engineers are the technical arm of the sales process, providing demos and technical support through the engagement. Their technical orientation makes them seem more trustworthy to prospects, so "sales" is never a part of their title and they never talk about price or contract terms with prospects.

This section of the playbook also articulates the interactions each role has with others in the organization, expectations for service level agreements, and other rules of engagement. For example:

- When a new customer signs a contract, the Sales Executive has 365 days to upsell or cross-sell more into the account. On day 366, the install base seller will be the sole seller in the account.

- When a customer has canceled their contract, the install base seller will have 365 days to try to renew them. If unsuccessful, the account will be treated as a "new logo prospect" for the BDR and Sales Executive team on day 366.

- When a BDR has set an appointment for a seller, the seller must accept or reschedule the meeting within 24 hours.

- When a BDR has created an appointment at an account, it will automatically be turned into an opportunity 48 hours following the meeting, unless the seller rejects it in CRM (along with a reason code) during that time.

The Customer Lifecycle

These roles and rules of engagement start to identify who a customer will interact with in our company for which purposes. Yet they only address those in the Go-To-Market organization who are users of the Sales Playbook. Outside of the sales process, customers will interact with our helpdesk, our billings and collections teams, our customer success managers, and many more. It's important for the GTM team to also understand these professionals' roles and responsibilities.

For example, customer success managers are responsible for ensuring our products are used by clients, and that they are happy with our services. They are not quota-carrying. Their measures of success are customer adoption and net promoter score, which is why they're not a part of the GTM organization. In the course of their interaction with customers, though, they may uncover the need to purchase additional products – and will bring in account managers to lead the evaluation and purchase of those tools.

The documentation of these interactions through the overall customer lifecycle, then, is a key section to include in our Sales Playbook.

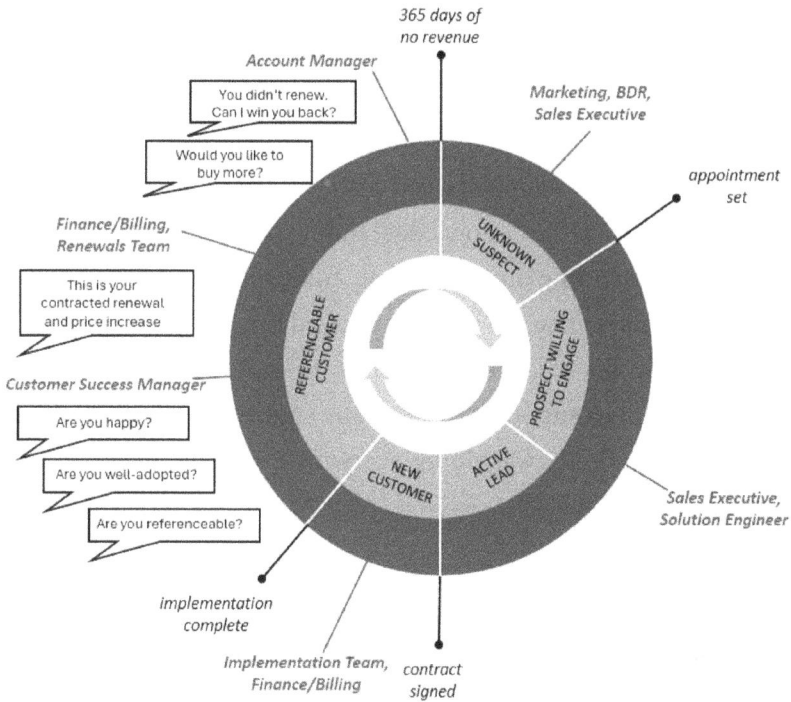

Fig 6.1: The Customer Lifecycle Involves Many Professionals from Many Parts of the Organization

My career has often involved building sales teams in organizations that were recently founder-led startups but have suddenly grown through merger or acquisition to become very large companies. When they were a small organization that could all fit within a single, collocated office, these roles and responsibilities were often vague. The entire company was perhaps a hundred very smart people who interacted with one another multiple times a day, and they just got things done for their couple hundred clients.

When these organizations suddenly have thousands of clients served by teams around the world, things get much more complicated. I worked in one organization that had a VP of Sales who used to know every customer personally and who was often the first person they'd call when they had a question or problem. He was technical enough and connected enough that he could often log into the customer's system on his own to fix their issues.

When the company suddenly merged with a competitor, nobody else in the organization had this knowledge about customer configurations. Worse, he was spending so much time continuing to maintain these existing customers that he wasn't able to spend time coaching new sellers on winning new ones. Other executives from product development started stepping in to support the solutions engineering team in demos, and suddenly everybody was doing everyone else's job, with very little time spent on their own.

Aligning the right person to the right job with the right expectations was one of the most important things that we did operationally for this team, and documenting it on a single sheet of paper—like the graphic in Figure 6.1—was critical to making it happen. That's why the customer lifecycle descriptions don't just belong in the Sales Playbook, but should also be duplicated in the playbooks of other teams who interact with the customer (support, customer success, finance, etc.).

The Lead Generation Process

The Sales Playbook will go into much more detail than this one-page graphic can provide. It describes the individual tasks for each discrete part of the customer lifecycle that the go-to-market team is involved in.

For example, the lead generation process is a prospect's first entry point into the customer lifecycle—and it's a complex one. Thinking back to our chapter on SMarketing, the playbook should specify who is responsible for which activities, with which personas, and which accounts to make sure the process is as efficient and effective as it can be.

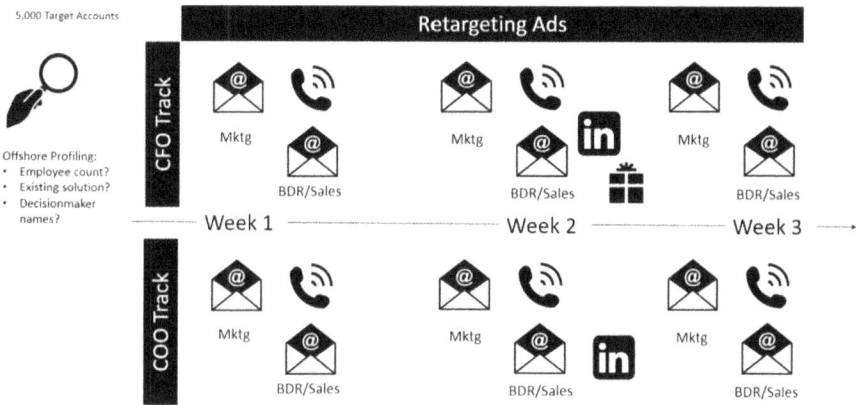

Fig 6.2: A Sales Playbook Defines how Multiple People Coordinate Activity to Generate Leads

The Sales Methodology

In our customer lifecycle, a lot of folks in the organization understand that "the sales team is working with the prospect after a lead has been generated." Yet there's a lot of complexity inside that black box of activity, and our sales methodology describes what's going on there, too. There are multiple sales methodologies that your company might choose, and whichever one you land on should be documented in the playbook.

Over the years, I've gravitated toward a variation of the MEDDIC sales process developed by PTC in the 1990s. My variation identifies nine questions that I believe need to be answered in every deal in order to result in a win, and has taken on the acronym MEDDPICCS. I may not have been consciously aware of it at the time, but in thousands of deals during decades of selling, I've never been able to win an opportunity where the customer didn't answer each of these questions for themselves. Helping my sellers to proactively, explicitly drive answers to these questions, then, is the core of the methodology I use.

They are:

Metrics: What are the quantifiable metrics by which we'll define our return on investment?

Economic Buyer: Who is the executive who will ultimately find the budget for our solution?

Decision Process: What are the steps this organization will go through to make a purchasing decision?

Decision Criteria: What will be the criteria, formal or informal, that they use to make a purchasing decision?

Paper Process: How does a contract ultimately get reviewed, redlined, and approved?

Identified Pain and Urgency: What is the compelling event that is driving a decision?

Champion/Partner: Who will use their influence to drive a decision in our favor?

Competition: What alternatives are we competing against, including "do nothing"?

Security: What technical review(s) do we need to pass in order to get their IT department to approve our product?

When the answers to each of these questions line up in our favor, we will have won the deal. We'll have identified a compelling pain that the organization has decided to address, the right people have weighed in on their options, and they've decided to allocate budget to selecting us above all others to drive towards a measurable result. Conversely, when any of these questions don't have an answer, the deal isn't ready to sign. We may be having a lot of conversations, or doing a lot of demos, but there is still selling work to do to get the deal done.

Stages and Exit Criteria

By definition, then, we spend the majority of our sales time without these answers in place. Our job as sellers is to use each selling moment as an opportunity to get one or more of them answered in our favor.

To guide that work, my Sales Playbook identifies a multi-step process to use that will systematically resolve each of the nine questions in as efficient a manner as possible. Like sales methodologies, there are many different sales processes your organization might adopt, and the specifics of the product you're selling may dictate unique steps that aren't used by anyone else.

Some organizations win when they offer a partial deployment or free trial for a period of time that automatically rolls into a contract if not canceled. Others avoid hands-on pilots at all costs. You might know that your team always wins if you can convince the client that a specific differentiated feature is critically important, or that a member of your executive team needs to connect with a key buying persona at a critical moment. Each of these steps is advancing an answer to one of the questions in the sales methodology.

Whatever the specifics of your process, defined sales stages help guide sellers through them. The playbook's definition of stages gives guidance to sellers on what they need to be doing with their prospect at any given point in time. Defined exit criteria help keep everyone aligned on what has already happened and what is yet to come.

Your stage definitions and exit criteria might look something like this:

Stage 1: Engage

In this stage, we are beginning to engage with a qualified lead and uncover their pain.

Methodology Questions to Answer: Identified Pain and Urgency.

Exit Criteria: Confirm that the customer sees the pain you've identified and is open to actively evaluating a solution.

Stage 2: Discover

In this stage, we are discovering more about the unique circumstances of the prospect's situation.

Methodology Questions to Answer: Economic Buyer, Decision Process.

Exit Criteria: Collaborate with the prospect to develop a Joint Evaluation Plan that identifies the steps involved in their evaluation process, names the various individuals involved in each step, and provides an ideal timeline for each step's completion.

Stage 3: Evaluate

In this stage, we are working with the prospect as they evaluate our solution.

Methodology Questions to Answer: Decision Criteria, Champion, Competition.

Exit Criteria: Conduct a solution demonstration, provide a directional ROI calculation, and review/update our Joint Evaluation Plan with them.

Stage 4: Propose

In this stage, we are delivering a specific proposal to the prospect.

Methodology Questions to Answer: Metrics, Paper Process.

Exit Criteria: Refine ROI calculation according to the prospect's preferred metrics. Provide a pricing proposal and standard contract template for review. Review and update our Joint Evaluation Plan with the prospect.

Stage 5: Secure

In this stage, we confirm that we are the prospects' vendor of choice, and eliminate barriers to completing the deal.

Methodology Questions to Answer: Security.

Exit Criteria: Complete any IT approvals their team requires. Confirm the remaining steps on the Joint Evaluation Plan are all that is left to do.

Stage 6: Negotiate

In this stage, we are negotiating the final price and redlining contracts with the prospect.

Exit Criteria: A contract has been agreed to and signed by the prospect.

Stage 7: Closed/Won

Our sales process is over, and we are handing over the new customer to the implementation and billing teams.

or

Stage 7: Closed/Lost or Closed/No Decision

If we've decided at any of the previous stages that the deal is not advancing to a win, it may advance to this stage, where we disengage, or begin nurturing the account as a new prospect again.

Many times, I've had deals get to Stage 4, and something seriously changes the course of the prospect's evaluation. Perhaps a key decisionmaker has left the company, or they've decided to put the project on hold for six months as they digest a recently-acquired company. In these instances, sellers may want to revert stages, moving them back to Stage 3 in our CRM system.

In these instances, I prefer to advance the opportunity to Stage 7, Closed/No Decision, as a more accurate representation of what has happened. When they pick up their project again, or the decision maker's replacement is found, we are probably going to have to revisit every step of the process with them from pain identification onward. Closing this opportunity and opening a fresh one helps us to be clear with ourselves on the status of the deal. It also helps us have a clean dataset to analyze questions like, "How many times do we go through a sales process with a customer before we get a win?" and, "What is the stage or activity that we tend to lose from most frequently?" so we can make refinements.

The Joint Evaluation Plan

Throughout the process, I've made reference to a Joint Evaluation Plan (JEP). This is a documented project plan that we regularly review with the prospect to make sure that we both agree on the various steps we'll be going through in their evaluation.

By agreeing to a JEP early in the sales process, I tell my prospects that they're not agreeing to purchase the product, but they're agreeing to the process by which we'll both invest our time and effort to determine if they will.

Things will absolutely change, but when I get a request for a second, third, or eighth demonstration, I can go back to the JEP and ask, "How does this additional demonstration advance us down the critical path of your evaluation?" We may find that there's a new decision maker involved that needs to be brought up to speed, which is great information as we resolve the nine questions of our methodology. Or, we may find that there's no real reason at all other than the customer has gotten stuck in their decision and doesn't know what else to do, which may lead us back to a review of the Pain, Metrics, ROI, or something other than the demo they requested.

When introducing a JEP, I always provide a template to start from which includes all stages of my sales process, explaining that "this may be the first time you've evaluated a solution like this, but it's the hundredth/thousandth time I've been through it, and these have generally been important steps each time." However, it's critical to then adapt and augment the JEP with whatever the customer shares about their own process. This is why the word "Joint" is in the title—it is something we build collaboratively together.

Many times, I've seen sellers miss this distinction, and proceed down the sales path with a JEP that says the contract will be signed on June 30th for no reason other than it's the last day of our quarter, and they're hoping it will be true. Meeting after meeting goes by where the seller flashes their hopeful JEP up on the screen without inviting comment, and the customer sits silently, knowing there is no way it's going to happen that way. Eventually, June 30th comes and goes, and the seller is panicking about what's going on in the deal they've been forecasting to their management team.

When we jointly create a plan with our prospects and continually test the dates and assumptions in them, we uncover all sorts of nuances about our deals. A prospect may tell us that a purchase of this size has to get approved by a budget committee that only meets on the third Thursday of every other month, so June 30th isn't at all a possibility, but July 18th absolutely is so long as we show up with their IT assessment forms already completed and signed off by their security team.

These situations are why devoting a section of our playbook to teaching sellers how to develop, talk about, and refine a JEP with their prospects is space well spent.

Personas

Much of the playbook I've described so far has been on the general, mechanical elements of a business. Yet, sellers also need very specific coaching on how to engage with their prospects around the specifics of the products being sold.

The Personas section introduces them to the key types of people they'll encounter in the client's organization. It helps them to identify key characteristics, typical pain points, and buying habits of these personas, along with the specific messaging your sellers should use to engage with them. This section likely contains customer stories to share about how a similar persona in a similar industry used your product to solve their pain and achieve a positive return on investment. Together, the components of this section help your team to gain credibility with their prospect, tailor their value proposition, and anticipate any objections or concerns that may arise.

Objection Handling and Competition

When I visit my sellers in their offices, I'm most likely to see their spiral-bound copy of the playbook opened to this section. It contains one-page overviews of each of our competitors' offerings, along with point-by-point comparisons of our strengths and weaknesses against them. Moreover, it provides specific words to say to address a variety of objections the customer may raise, as well as the seeds of Fear, Uncertainty, and Doubt we can plant in their mind to weaken our competition's position.

Sales Plays

Get a Sales Playbook
Template at

bit.ly/3Z1wvmy

This is another frequently-visited section of the playbook, providing one-page guidance for sellers to execute against common situations in deals. It's the collection of best practices that don't really fit elsewhere in the book but that our best sellers have internalized.

You'll have plenty of topics to include in this section, but some of my favorites include:

- Give to Get: How to use a customer request for something to get the information we want

- Multi-threading Accounts: How to bring more decision-makers to the table without alienating our coach

- Executive Alignment: How to get the attention of a key executive who hasn't been participating in the process

- Pricing Pivot: How to defer early questions about pricing to a time after the prospect believes in the value we provide

- Providing References: The who and how of introducing key customers into this sales cycle

- Testing Your Champion: Ways to evaluate how much influence your champion really has

- Sandler's Pendulum: How to re-introduce momentum into stalled deals

- I Happen to Be in Town: Using a spontaneous trip to jump-start a stalled deal

- Rejecting Unwanted Trials: How to respond to requests for "a test drive"

Tools and Job Aides

The final section of the playbook includes worksheets, tools, and job aides that help your sellers do their jobs. It will include JEP templates, ROI calculators, and step-by-step walkthroughs of how to use your internal systems (CRM, quote builders, etc.). It's a jumping-off point that my front-line managers use as they coach their sellers through skills. The toolbox contains a wide variety of items that can be pulled out and used to address just about any specific situation a seller may encounter.

CHAPTER 7

The Annual Sales Kickoff

I have an unusually-large collection of blue shoes. Blue Converse high-tops. Metallic blue patent leather shoes. Dress shoes with bright blue bottoms. Blue suede shoes. If they're blue and can be found on Amazon for under $50, I've got them.

The collection began at a sales kickoff for a company that had recently merged two competitors together, and had unified under a bright blue logo. To keep reminding our sellers of this new brand, I put on a new pair of blue shoes for every event we had across a week of kickoff events. There were so many blue shoes, they filled an entire suitcase that was so large it had to be checked under the plane to get to and from the meeting.

Sellers took notice. They began stopping me in the hotel lobby to get a better look at them. And the next time we got together, many showed up with blue shoes of their own, posting pictures of them on LinkedIn with our new brand's hashtag. The shoes became part of a signature style for the rest of my tenure at that company, and I think it survives in the culture there, many years since I've left.

When we begin a year, we start with an annual plan that we believe we can achieve. We've got a playbook that describes how to get there, and we've got a team in place that we like and believe can execute against it. But we also need to be sure our sellers believe in the plan, believe in their part of it, and are energized to tackle the long year ahead. Their quotas have been reset to zero, so whether a seller made a lot of money the year before or none at all, each one is looking at their territory, their pipeline, and their commission plan and deciding whether to continue to invest time with us.

Hosting an inspirational kickoff event with many memorable moments that remind folks about your plan to help them succeed is your best opportunity to win the hearts and minds of your sellers for another year.

In-Person or Virtual

For years, sales kickoff has been an in-person event. The COVID pandemic forced a lot of these to go virtual in 2020 and 2021, and, impressed with the cost savings, a lot of CFOs have encouraged them to remain online ever since. While I'm proud of the virtual kickoffs I produced during that time, I'm a strong advocate for an in-person event.

Poor uptake of your training will make it hard for sellers to succeed. Failing to inspire and motivate your best sellers will result in costly turnover and empty territories as you recruit replacements. Being together in-person for a few days creates opportunities for thousands of impromptu interactions while passing in a hallway, sharing a meal, or enjoying entertainment that can't really be replicated online. And while the costs of being in person may be high, the costs of having a poor kickoff are even higher.

If you've got a sales team of any size, you'll want to select and book your kickoff venue about a year in advance. January and February are the most common times for company meetings and hotels that can accommodate hundreds or thousands of attendees get booked quickly. Once you've secured your contract with them, publish the date to your sellers so that everyone knows far in advance when and where they're expected to be and can plan accordingly.

Even with a year's notice, there will be some sellers who can't make your event. People get married, have babies, or have commitments with their families that will make it impossible for every member of a team to attend in person. For this reason, I strongly encourage you to have each key portion of your event live-streamed and recorded for future playback. It shouldn't be broadly advertised as an optional way to participate. You want every seller to do their best at your physical kickoff to gain all of the benefits that can only happen with in-person participation. But given the choice of "not attending at all" and having a sub-par online experience, you should have an online experience for those who legitimately can't join you at your kickoff hotel.

Timing

Ideally, a kickoff happens in the second or third week of your new year. It's far enough past the end of the last year that everyone is back to work, but early enough that what you do at kickoff can still influence the course of the quarter and the year.

If you've delivered comp plans, quotas, and territories on the first day of the year (which you should), your teams will have digested them, and you should be starting to get feedback from the field about what they like and don't like about them. Having kickoff a few weeks later gives you time to adjust your messaging and respond to concerns before sellers get so entrenched in their thinking that they've already decided to leave.

Producing a high-quality event takes a lot of preparation. You should have defined your main messages and outlined the event no later than the first week of Q4. You should have your speakers' content locked in before the quarter is over, leaving spaces to fill in the blanks for final revenue attainment and the complete list of sellers who achieved the quota. The first two weeks of the year leading up to the event itself, then, are largely about rehearsing your speakers to ensure they deliver your message perfectly.

Choosing A Theme

Kickoff is an inspiring and educational event, and you want your attendees to remember it throughout the year. You likely have two or three really big takeaways you want attendees to absorb during the meeting, whether that be excitement about implementing a new sales technique, enablement on a new product you've brought to market, or something else. Choose a theme for your event that summarizes them all into a pithy word or phrase. Ideally, one that can serve as a theme for the entire year, morphing and twisting as the quarters unfold.

One year, I joined a company that had a music-related name and whose sales team needed to show more courage and swagger in their approach to the market. Skills training was going to be focused on giving my early-thirties sellers the confidence to call senior executives at Fortune 500 companies with a serious ROI message. A competitor had recently done a splashy re-brand that claimed our user interface was old and tired, and our teams needed to be reminded that we still had the superior solution. We themed kickoff "forte," the musical term for playing loudly and boldly, and tied it into everything we did.

Always a fan of an object lesson, I put hand-held drums, tambourines, and noisemakers on outdoor dinner tables one night, and brought in a percussionist to guide my 150 attendees through "making some noise," which culminated in a surprise noisy fireworks display. I saw those toy instruments in people's offices for years afterward, and am still known as "the forte fireworks guy" to a certain class of sellers.

Another year, I was working with a team that was turning the page on poor performance. Almost nobody had made quota the year before, and they were starting this new year with next to no pipeline. It was clearly going to be a year of rebuilding, and so "Acceleration" became our theme. At kickoff, we talked about how tiny a snowball may look at the top of a hill, but how very large and fast it can grow over time, making a huge impact by the time it reaches the bottom. At regional gatherings, teams went go-kart racing or visited the Indianapolis speedway. Halfway through the year, we revisited the theme even as we celebrated our "momentum" and got track star and nine-time Olympic medalist Carl Lewis to record a video for our sellers about continuing to speed towards the finish line.

Agenda Management

Most kickoff events last between two and five days. No matter how much time you allocate to yours, it will never feel like enough. As soon as they hear that the entire sales team will be together in one room, people from across the company will start asking if they can have a speaking slot to talk about a wide variety of topics.

My colleagues are used to hearing me say that "Kickoff is the most expensive thing we will do all year." It's certainly a big cash outlay in hotel rooms, meeting technology, food, and entertainment - but it's even more expensive because we are dedicating the time of every seller to it for an extended period. There is opportunity cost for them being out of the field and selling, and they also tend to be the most highly-paid people in the company. For all of these reasons, it doesn't take a very large team to make every minute cost tens of thousands of dollars.

With this in mind, I also remind everyone that the event is about our sellers and their needs. I'm very thoughtful about which topics make the cut by looking at every topic request and considering what objective we're trying to advance by including it.

"What do we want our sellers to be able to do immediately following the session?" and "How will this session help us to sell more in the coming year?" are great questions to qualify content in or out, especially when they're weighted against "Is it worth spending ten thousand dollars a minute to deliver?" Topic proposals along the lines of, "I want our Sellers to know X" are not sufficient for a kickoff presentation. Most of those goals can be addressed with an email, a Zoom, or something outside of this event.

Many topics and speakers will seem important but must be weighed against the outcomes we expect to achieve from our kickoff investment, and then only allow those that reinforce our biggest messages and goals. For those who do deserve time on the main stage, allocate that time wisely. Does a speaker really need 30 whole minutes to deliver their content, or could it be achieved in 20, or 15 instead?

As a seller, I attended way too many kickoff events where the CEO was given 60 minutes "to talk to the team about what's on their mind," and rambled, contradicted the teaching and advice that was given the rest of the week, and went 15 minutes overtime—causing another session to be skipped entirely or keeping everyone grumbling in their seats that the whole meeting ran late. I vowed as a CRO that I would never let this happen under my own watch. That's why I don't allow anyone to present at my kickoff unless I've personally seen and approved their content many weeks ahead of time, and know that it advances my meeting objective.

While it's sometimes uncomfortable to tell a new CEO that they won't be allowed on my kickoff stage unless we've reviewed their content three weeks earlier or that I've decided they really only need 15 minutes to deliver the message they want to convey, it's ultimately led to a much crisper, more effective event for everyone involved.

Time Management

As you plan the flow of the week, be sure you're also allocating appropriate breaks throughout the meeting. People lose focus really quickly when they've been sitting in a conference room for any length of time. While you might possibly be able to keep their attention for a single 90-minute session for the very first event on the very first day, subsequent sessions should really only last 60 minutes apiece, and 45 is even better. As the week progresses, you might consider shifting your start time progressively later each day—from 8:30 to 8:45 and then to 9 am—to help your team feel less rushed and more prepared for the day.

Mid-session breaks should last at least 15 minutes, and even up to 30, giving attendees enough time to go back to their rooms quickly to grab a sweater, have a snack, visit the restroom, and ideally have a meaningful conversation with a colleague before coming back into the meeting. Lunch breaks might extend to 90 minutes, both for the logistics of moving a large crowd through a meal, but also to give your teams time to catch up on email, make important phone calls, or do other business that will allow them to come back to your next session without any distractions.

Returning from break will take more time than you expect. A friend of mine works at a four thousand-seat performing arts center in Chicago and offered me last-minute tickets to a concert one evening. I jumped in the car right away but got stuck in traffic and wasn't walking through the theater doors until the clock was just striking eight. My friend greeted me in the lobby and asked if I wanted to grab a quick cocktail at the bar before we sat down. I said no, they're flashing the lights in the lobby. The show's about to begin, we don't have any time. Laughing, she explained they always hold the curtain for a few minutes after the posted show time because there will be dozens of people who still need to visit the bathroom, park the car, or do any number of things that will make them officially "late" to settle into their seats. We had a glass of champagne and took our seats right as the lights went down for the show to start—at ten past the hour. I always think of this experience as I plan meetings, and create a few minutes of "throwaway video content" wrapped in high production value to start each session which helps cover this delayed start time.

As soon as one session ends and we go to break, the screens in the room display a countdown timer with a message: "The next session will begin in 20 minutes." Five or seven minutes before the session is supposed to begin, meeting coordinators circulate through the lobby, ringing handheld chimes that indicate it's time to head back into the session. Right when the timer hits zero and the official session start time has arrived, we play a roughly three-minute video that is topical, but not critical if you missed it. Small video clips of customers saying how happy they are to work with us are interspersed with clips of fast runners, noisy drum lines, or other b-roll clips that reinforce whatever the theme of the meeting is. The video ends, the "Voice of God" comes over the loudspeaker saying, "Please welcome to the stage your Chief Revenue Officer, JD Miller," and I'm walking out to start the session about four minutes "late," with at least 50% more folks in the audience than were seated five minutes previously.

Manage Your Speakers Appropriately

The speakers themselves need to be effective in achieving their session objective and need to be able to do it in the time allowed.

Some topical experts simply aren't effective in-person speakers. The lead engineer who wrote the code for the new product may have done really great work and might be recognized and thanked by name for their contribution, but if they're not also a dynamic presenter who is good at public speaking, they shouldn't be delivering the session to introduce their creation to the sales team. For every speaker, schedule a dry run of their content at least four weeks ahead of kickoff, giving you time to adjust content, format, or change out speakers if needed. Expect that most speakers will need more than one dry run to get their content packaged appropriately for the big event.

As you refine their presentations, make sure the speakers are highly attentive to the time they're taking to deliver their content. While the officially-published agenda may say that they're leading a 20-minute session, the returning-from-break filler video means they actually only have 16 minutes. Make sure the speaker knows this in advance, has trimmed their slides down to fill the allotted time (certainly no more than one slide per minute), and has practiced with a stopwatch to make sure it all fits together.

For the event itself, have your AV team put a "confidence monitor" at the foot of the stage that shows the speaker their presentation notes alongside a countdown timer indicating how much time they have left. It should change color and start flashing red when they have five minutes left, and when there's less than one minute to go, your MC (or you, if you're acting in that capacity) needs to start heading to the stage, graciously moving them off and introducing the next speaker. Just like the Oscars, playing transition music and cutting off their microphone may be helpful.

The week of the event, set aside time for each presenter to have a technical practice session on stage, ideally at least 24 hours before their official session. They don't need to practice their entire presentation but should do enough so that the AV team can test microphone placement and volume levels. The presenter should click through every slide to understand how the monitors and tools work, and confirm that every build and animation runs as expected. No further changes should be made to presentation materials after this time.

Variety, Variety, Variety

Today's professionals are highly influenced by their use of social and digital media and have shorter attention spans than they did ten years ago. We can engage this group effectively by interspersing video clips to highlight key points and break up the monotony of a presentation.

Here, too, time management and judicious editing are key. I've seen sales leaders present clips from the movie "Glengarry Glen Ross" more times than I can count, usually after watching them click around YouTube for a minute or two as they search for the "Coffee is for Closers scene." I've seen the 7-minute and 15-second clip of the scene, the 3-minute and 22-second clip, and the 18-second clip. Guess which was most effective? If you're using any video that you didn't create yourself, recognize that you can—and usually should—trim it down shorter than whatever length you received it in. Also, be sure to pay the appropriate usage royalties to the party that created the content you're using.

Video is especially useful to deliver a prerecorded demonstration of new products. Invariably, live demos are ground to a halt when the presenter suddenly realizes that their laptop doesn't have the right connection point to the presentation screens, or the internet goes down, or any number of other glitches. A streamlined demo that cuts out time "waiting for a report to load" or navigating through multiple clicks to get from one screen to another will have much more impact.

Another way to create variety is to change the size of the audience, moving them to different locations throughout the day to keep their interest engaged. Perhaps the largest announcements and topics are covered in the morning as big mainstage addresses, while teams go to smaller breakout rooms in the afternoon for detailed training or skills-based roleplays.

In the context of the mainstage, it's also helpful to give attendees something new to look at each time they return to the room. Work with your AV and event operations teams to change the lighting and rearrange the stage furniture during every break. Have some sessions delivered from a podium, giving other topics a "fireside chat" or talk-show format with two or three speakers in chairs around a table. Break up hour-long sessions into micro-sessions so that the topic or speaker changes every ten minutes or so, or use interactive tools to take quick polls of the audience who text a number or scan a QR code to provide real-time feedback on a topic.

Props and giveaways are also great ways to reinforce your message while creating variety for your attendees. When I was an individual contributor, I attended a kickoff where the main message our CRO wanted us to leave with was, "The company depends on all of us doing our part to achieve its goal. So, it's important for every seller to close at least one thing—even a tiny add-on product—every quarter."

He played a clip from the movie Vertical Limit, where a family is rock climbing, using ropes and belay devices as they make their way up the mountain. An accident happens, and one by one, each of the safety devices pops out of the rock, until the entire family is hanging on a single rope, threaded through a single carabiner, and attached to the mountain in one place. He went on to explain that we could think of each deal we closed as a single carabiner, never knowing which one would be the critical one for our collective success. As we went into the lobby for break, each seller was given a carabiner for each consecutive quarter they'd closed at least one deal.

More than 20 years later, I still clearly remember the enormous chains of carabiners that some of our sellers wore the rest of the week, and the embarrassment of others who had only one or no carabiners to carry around.

Important Kickoff Events

In addition to product launches, messaging updates, and training, I've collected a few "must have" sessions to include in all of my kickoffs.

Invite-Only Pre-Event Reception

The night before the kickoff officially begins, I host a small reception with other executive team members for a select group of employees who have received an invitation hand-written by me prior to the event.

I invite all "top performers" (whether or not they all quite achieved 100% of quota), who enjoy having an opportunity for one-on-one interaction with our executive team in an intimate setting. While the event is not published on the public agenda, word definitely gets around about this exclusive event, and other sellers set goals to have a strong enough performance to get invited to next year's reception.

New hires are also invited to the event. They're still assimilating to the organization and trying to decide if they've made the right choice by writing the next chapter of their career with us, and the small group setting allows them to build connections with one another, with our executive team, and with their best-performing colleagues. In years when budgets are larger, these guests might return to their room after this event to find a small gift left for them with another handwritten note that looks forward to a successful year together.

Diversity and Affinity Groups

In large organizations, we tend to get a critical mass of folks who might be under-represented in smaller sales teams, and they enjoy having a chance to connect with one another to talk about issues specific to their subgroup.

I celebrate having a diverse sales team and often use it as a differentiator in the recruiting process. Kickoff is a great time to support these groups by giving them an opportunity to gather with one another at some point during the week. Setting aside a small dining room during one of the larger lunch breaks has worked very well, with one day's lunch providing a venue for

"Women in Sales," another day for "LGBTQ+ Sellers," and a third for "BIPOC Sellers." Increasingly, I've had strong sellers who identify with all three groups, and who attend every one of these optional events.

Beyond ensuring that there is a space for them to meet and asking for a rough headcount during the registration process, these events often require little additional planning. The teams typically like to self-organize their agendas, which are open to anyone who identifies with the affinity group, as well as their friends and allies.

Commission Plan Office Hours

Team members will have received copies of their variable compensation plans a few weeks before kickoff, and often will have questions about them. At one breakfast during the week, I like to set aside rooms for drop-in questions about the plan. Recognizing that the commission plan for quota-carrying sellers may be different than the plan for solutions engineers, a separate room is designated as the place to go for questions on each team's plan and is staffed by finance or sales leadership team members who are familiar with that particular plan.

These ad-hoc environments provide a great opportunity to teach your sellers how to "work their plan" for maximum payout. If you designed the plan correctly, it also maximizes the likelihood of them performing the behaviors you want to see this year. Come prepared with some specific examples to walk through about how their commission payout might change when you adjust deal length, add specific new products, or do whatever else it is that you're emphasizing in your plan this year.

Unstructured Work Time

It can be hard for anyone to be out of the field for a few days, and team members will appreciate having 90-120 minutes at some point during the week when they can schedule customer calls, catch up on email or organize random meetings with one another. Publish this block of time in your agenda and circulate it well ahead of kickoff, so that sellers can offer it as availability to their prospects in the weeks leading up to your event.

Tech and Administrative Support

With increasingly-virtual teams, the sales kickoff is often the only time a seller may get in-person access to your corporate staff. Consider setting up an IT helpdesk for them to get annoying laptop issues repaired or troubleshoot recurring concerns. Similarly, consider having an administrative helpdesk where employees can get assistance with modifying flights home, request a forgotten toothbrush, or otherwise get support on tactical issues that will make them better able to participate in the week.

Team Building Activities

One of the most important parts of kickoff is the opportunity to have people in the same room together, strengthening their interpersonal relationships. Shared experiences outside of structured training time can be a key part of making that happen. This is a part of kickoff that a lot of companies don't give thoughtful attention to. They have unstructured time in their agenda, and assume most people will spend it together in the hotel bar. That's often a recipe for disaster. Someone drinks too much, poor decisions are made, and someone loses their job as a result, and it's often one of your top revenue producers.

Rather than having events that are focused on alcohol, I like to create social opportunities around volunteerism. No matter where your kickoff is held, there's likely to be a local organization that will bring an activity to you, whether that be stuffing backpacks with school supplies, sorting and folding clothes for a homeless services organization, putting together toys for a local nursery school, or something else. All of these activities can be done in a hotel ballroom with wine and appetizers to accompany them, but shifting the focus to volunteerism creates a much better vibe. As an added bonus, your finance team may find a way to take a charitable deduction for some of the costs of the event.

I've also found great success in offering an optional morning workout or yoga session as a way to build energy at the start of the day. Many of my younger salespeople are also certified personal trainers or yoga instructors, and they enjoy having the opportunity to interact with colleagues in a different format than usual.

Awards and Recognition

Salespeople are a competitive bunch, and most crave public recognition in front of their peers. I underestimated the importance of this until I spoke with a top performer who told me he would rather receive a trophy than a $5k bonus. Thinking he was an anomaly, I asked the rest of the millennial first-time sellers on the team, whose junior status made them the lowest-paid quota carriers in the company. All agreed with this sentiment.

I quickly found an online resource that sold five-foot tall, customizable trophies for under $75, and began handing them out, with a small wrench to disassemble them in order to fit into carry-on luggage, at every sales meeting. The team was ecstatic. These trophies became such a part of the culture at that company that a seller who unfortunately chose to leave for another job used their exit interview to remind our HR team that they'd recently qualified for a quarterly award, and wanted to be sure we had the correct shipping address for their trophy.

With this in mind, I reserve my final night at kickoff for an awards dinner, where we recognize and celebrate top performances from the past year, and I give out as many trophies as possible. Solutions Engineer of the Year, Rookie of the Year, First BDR to Set 20 Appointments In 100

Days in Louisiana … All of these are potential celebrations, alongside the traditional top revenue producers and quota achievers of the prior year.

"Club" Qualifiers

The awards night culminates in the recognition of sellers who have achieved your "Club" status for the year, whether that be 100% quota attainment or other qualification threshold. Each is named individually and called up on stage, followed by a short video that describes the fantastic vacation destination they'll be traveling to.

When I qualified for my first Club trip, I was given a small candy dish carved from a coconut tree and engraved with the words "LexisNexis Circle of Excellence" at that awards night, as I heard about a luxury getaway at a five-star resort on an island beach.

The fact that I still keep that dish on my desk nearly 25 years later tells me it was a milestone event in my selling career, so I try to find a similar small gift for my Club qualifiers to receive at kickoff as part of their recognition.

Get a Sample Kickoff Agenda at

bit.ly/3yQtCug

The night closes with a final sizzle reel that unveils wherever the next Club trip will be. It's accompanied by a statement like "Mark your calendars. This is where I'm going in about 15 months, and I want every one of you to be standing on stage with me next year to celebrate that you're coming too. You'll get there by succeeding this year. And it's completely in your control. You all have a blank slate in front of you, and have all received the skills and tools this week that will get you there. Let's all put them to great use." It's a great final note to finish the kickoff event.

Announcing a Club trip a year in advance is hard work. Your finance team will be anxious about putting down a large cash deposit for a trip to a luxury destination when they don't know how your year is going to turn out, and it is tricky to negotiate with the destination when you don't know quite how many people will be going on the trip.

If you're at an organization that has a company-wide Peak Performers Trip instead of a Sales-Only Club, you'll have to coordinate with HR. And it means you'll have to do site visits and select a destination three months before kickoff in order to announce the trip that people will take three months after your next one. Yet, being able to give your sellers a specific target to hit, with a specific date and destination in mind, is great motivation and worth the work.

Other Notes

A few other secrets that I've picked up over the years that have made kickoff work especially well for me include:

Repeat It Quarterly. Unless you're a very small team at a company that is innovating at a really fast rate, you're unlikely to plan a multi-day, in-person kickoff every quarter. Yet it's good to regularly return to the skills and lessons that you taught during your start of the year event, celebrating where they've been used successfully, and adjusting where they're not working as well. I've found that two, 60-minute Zoom meetings (with a 15-minute break in between) work well for an abbreviated, quarterly kickoff event.

Work with your creative teams to have great interactive video content, and use the same event branding that you did at the start of the year, continuing to reinforce that overarching annual theme. If budget allows, ship a package to every participant that has some interactive element they can use to reinforce the message (this is a great time to add extra links to those carabiner chains), or encourage small-group "viewing parties" in local offices or where clusters of team members live. Encourage them to go out for a team lunch or dinner afterward to continue building their sense of camaraderie.

Know Everybody. My sales teams see me present a lot, know a lot of my idiosyncrasies, and of course know me by name as their CRO. It's natural for them to assume, then, that I know them just as well – though often, teams are way too large to make that feasible. I cover with a few tricks:

- **Nametags.** At check-in, give every attendee a lanyard with a nametag where their first name is printed large enough to be read from 20 feet away (this font size was getting bigger every year until surgery returned me to 20/20 vision). Last name and home town can be printed in smaller font, and name tag color might indicate whether they are a seller, solutions engineer, sales ops professional, or something else. You'll encourage team members to wear them all week by printing a QR code on the back that will take them to the week's agenda, with all locations, breaks, and other details they need.

- **Photo books.** A few weeks before the event, I ask each of my front-line managers to identify any of their team members who have something particularly special I should know about and reference in my interaction with them – a new baby, a particularly hard-won deal, and so on. Those comments get printed alongside a photo taken from their LinkedIn profile and put into a photo book that I print and study on the plane on my way to the event. Throughout the week, I check in with the book and commit five of them to short-term memory, so that I can seek them out and have the right conversation before the next session begins.

- **Trusted Colleagues.** I've also confided in my executive assistant and close operations colleagues that I need help remembering each of these details. One of them is usually within eyesight, and we've worked out a signal where I can let them know to be on the lookout for any of the folks I need to interact with, or could use their help refreshing my memory of who I'm talking with at the moment.

Stay Energized. Delivering inspirational presentations for three straight days, attending the earliest morning breakfasts, and being available for the group in the lobby who wants to have one last conversation over a drink before going to bed is physically taxing. A few things have kept me at the top of my game:

- Sleep well the week before kickoff, minimizing travel if at all possible.

- Arrive at the kickoff venue a day before anyone else is expected, to get time to rest and settle in for a long week.

- Identify time on the agenda when I can get a light workout in each day – even if it's just a 15 minute session that I can sneak in while everyone else is in small breakout rooms.

- Hydrate. I can never drink too much water. Or Diet Coke.

- Limit Alcohol. While there will be occasional relationships that can be further developed over a chat and a drink, kickoff is a long week that's tiring enough on its own. I'm likely to be drinking a club soda with lime at these gatherings.

Set Behavioral Expectations. Most sellers have stories about "that one person at their sales kickoff." They drank too much, were inappropriate with their colleagues, or spent all day at the pool instead of going to training. Unfortunately, there are any number of things that people can do in group settings that damage their professional reputations, or have resulted in immediate termination, even if they sold more than anyone else in the business. It's easy for these things to happen. Remote workers are excited to reconnect with colleagues they haven't seen in months, and fresh college grads are overwhelmed as they experience their first-ever business trips.

In the weeks leading up to the event, then, I ask my front line managers to have a casual talk in one of their team meetings about "not being that person." It doesn't need to be heavy-handed, but a quick reminder of a real-life story of kickoff behavior gone wrong generally reinforces the kind of culture we want to create and gets everyone in the right mindset for a great trip together, with no collateral damage.

CHAPTER 8

Performance Improvement and the Weekly 1:1

I once worked for a CEO whose career brought him there through the finance ranks. More than most, he saw every issue as one of dollars and cents, and he taught every leader that they needed to delegate every task to the lowest-cost resource who could successfully do the work. Doing so would free up the leaders' time to work on the most complicated, most high-impact tasks that only they could solve, which included training and developing others so that there would be more than one individual in the organization who could do those tasks.

It can be a hard lesson to put into practice.

When video editing software became inexpensive enough to be run on a laptop computer, I was among the first group of professionals to embed multimedia into my routine work. Soon, I was producing quick videos to embed in email campaigns, or editing interviews with customers and employees for use in user conferences or internal meetings. It was new, and it got results. Prospects engaged with those emails more frequently than text-only ones, and colleagues complimented me on how engaging and inspiring our team meetings were becoming. And, being human, I responded to this positive feedback by doing more of it.

Over time, the rest of the world hopped on the video trend, and the stakes got higher. In order to keep up with the latest trends, I had to install a pop-up green screen in my home office. Animations, subtitles and multiple camera angles became standard expectations for our audiences, and I kept plowing ahead, further refining this skill that had differentiated me for so long.

One day, a trusted event planner offered to have her team produce some of the video content for a meeting we were putting together. I declined, reminding her that I was more than capable of doing the work myself and knowing that I'd get it exactly how I wanted it, too. She let it go, and we ran the meeting with video content I spent a few hours building. But the next time we had a meeting, she showed up with some video work pre-built as an example of what they could do. It was great—better than what I could do myself—and they'd produced it in much less time than I would have taken to produce something much less impressive. I got to spend more of my own meeting prep time working with the team of folks who would be leading training sessions, and I was able to identify and solve some problems in their content that I'd have missed if I was doing video editing.

The events team has produced all of the multimedia for my meetings ever since.

When you spend time thinking about whether you're the only person capable of doing a particular task, and then asking the follow-up question of whether you should be the only one who can do it, you'll soon have a long list of topics you want to train others to do immediately. Chapter 11 will talk about using in-field experiences and in-office Deal Clinics as two great tools for sales-specific skills development. But for the ongoing development of team members on a broad set of professional skills, a quarterly performance improvement plan and weekly one-on-one is the best toolset I know.

Grounding Development In A Plan

Get a Development Plan Template at

bit.ly/4dFvzZM

At the heart of the development process is a written development plan for each team member. At the beginning of each quarter, I meet with my direct reports to identify performance objectives for the next 90 days.

For sellers, most of these objectives flow directly from the annual plan. We'll identify the dollar amounts and number of deals they need to close over the next 90 days, along with the specific leading activities that will set them up for success in later quarters – the deal stage advancements, discovery calls, and prospecting activities that our Win Creation Waterfall identified. Each of these goals should be documented in a development plan, alongside the specific metric we will use to measure success in 90 days. These job-specific skills are half of the documented plan.

The other half is a professional development plan. Here, I have conversations with my direct reports around what they envision for their future career, and which skills they'll need to develop to get there. BDRs may want to become quota-carrying sellers, or may be more interested in a solutions engineering path. Quota carriers may want to lead teams, and front line managers may aspire to the c-suite.

Whatever the path, we document the necessary skills that need to be developed, along with a plan for how they might be gained. VPs might shadow me at my next board meeting, and a manager might take a business finance course at the local community college to learn how to read a P&L statement. All of these ideas get documented in the development plan, too.

Reviewing and Updating the Plan Quarterly

At the end of the quarter, we'll revisit this written development plan through a structured review process. First, I have the employee write a self-review to assess how they think they progressed on each item. Next, I write my own review. Finally, we collaborate on what the plan for the next 90 days should look like to continually grow their skills.

At the end of the year, most companies have an annual review process where they ask managers to rate each employee's performance against their objectives from the entire year, often giving them a rating of "exceeds expectations, meets expectations, or needs improvement." If we've been updating development plans, the annual review process should be simple. It's just a matter of combining the four quarterly checkpoints into a single document that reviews the full year's performance, and setting objectives for the next year.

As far as the formal annual review is concerned, only the first half of the development plan (the performance objectives section) should influence the employee's overall rating. An employee who is achieving all of their objectives, but not necessarily developing skills for a new job is "meeting expectations" or "exceeding expectations," depending on their results. Spending time on the professional development half of the plan, however, is what allows the employee to grow in their career, and often feel more satisfied in the organization.

The Performance Improvement Plan

Looked at objectively, this individual development plan is designed to continually improve performance. Ideally, we would call this document a "Performance Improvement Plan." Yet in many organizations, that plan (abbreviated as a PIP) has become shorthand for saying, "I'm giving my employee notice that I will fire them within 90 days."

That's unfortunate.

The "getting ready to fire an employee PIP" has a lot of similar characteristics to the development plan that I've described here. It documents a set of performance objectives with metrics that should be achieved over a specific time frame. It tells the employee that the manager will be reviewing those metrics with them in a defined time frame, and it warns the employee that if the performance standard isn't met, there may be consequences, including termination from their job.

Often, managers don't have performance conversations—or document these plans—until a team member's performance has gotten so bad that the manager has already decided to terminate them. The documentation and 90-day process, then, are just a bit of legal housekeeping that HR enforces in hopes of avoiding a wrongful termination lawsuit.

I was in my late twenties the first time I was the recipient of a PIP document of any kind. I'd never even heard of one, and had absolutely no idea that things weren't going well until my manager and the head of HR called me to a meeting, presenting me with a 90-day performance improvement plan, alongside a confidential separation agreement that essentially said we could skip the whole 90-day process if I'd accept a financial payment, agree to leave that day, and waive my right to sue. It was a devastating experience. It shattered my confidence for years, leaving me always worried I would be fired by surprise. Twenty-some years later, I still remember being fired in this way, and I still have no idea what I did (or didn't do) to cause it.

It was a lost opportunity for me to grow, learn, and develop. It was a lost opportunity for my employer, too. If my manager had been using a development plan as part of the routine cadence to operate the business, I'd potentially have been able to course correct before things had gotten to the point of no return. I might have become a successful contributor to the company, they wouldn't have had to pay the separation fee, and they also would have avoided the hard-dollar and productivity-loss costs of recruiting and onboarding my replacement (who, likely would have had a similarly-costly PIP process if the manager didn't start having ongoing development discussions with them, either).

Having a performance improvement or development plan in place for every employee that gets looked at every 90 days is a much better strategy, for everyone involved.

Weekly 1:1s

Writing a quarterly development plan makes you and your team perform better than if these ideas aren't put in writing. You'll be even better, though, if you use this written plan as the framework for a continuous development process. The core work of development happens in weekly one-on-one meetings between the front-line manager and their direct report.

The meeting agenda consists of looking at progress against the job performance metrics (this is closely tied to the pipeline review for sellers), checking in on progress against the professional development goals, and collaborative work together that advances one or more of those goals. I tell my own direct reports that a 30-minute one-on-one is a sacrosanct part of our relationship, and one that I expect them to have with each of their direct reports. It may get moved around during the week, but we should never have a week go by where we don't have this one-on-one meeting if we can at all help it.

Thirty minutes is a tight agenda. I often describe it as "ten minutes about the company goals, ten minutes about your goals, and ten minutes of working together on something." If it's the only time that I'm spending with my direct report, something is going wrong. I am usually leading virtual teams, so in practice, I have a pretty fluid ongoing interaction with each of my team members that unfolds in brief Slack or text exchanges, or ad-hoc phone calls throughout our day.

Still, knowing that we have a dedicated time set aside each week—every week—to pay attention to the important task of skills development means that my teams are getting some form of structured development that is better than I had in my late twenties. And whether you're a fresh-out-of-college BDR, a Senior VP with decades of experience, or even a member of the c-suite, there's no task more important than taking time to focus on continued growth and development.

A Dedicated Sales Enablement Team

When structuring my teams, I like to make sure that no manager has more than eight direct reports. With this ratio, assuming the manager did nothing else but coach team members all day, they would have one hour a day, every day, to devote to each team member's development.

In practice, of course, the manager is pulled into many other things, giving them less time to devote to talent development. That's why they shouldn't be the only person developing the talent of your sellers. Ideally, your organization has invested in a sales enablement team that is constantly thinking about how to raise the skill level of everyone in the go-to-market team, grounded in the lessons documented in your Sales Playbook.

The Onboarding Plan

Their work begins with a new hire onboarding plan. For every role in the organization, your enablement team should have thought about the critical skills needed to succeed, which should have already been documented and screened for in your recruiting process, as well as the specific tactical items a seller needs to master.

About 15 years ago, I went through the sales onboarding process at a Fortune 100 tech company. It involved flying to a remote city for two solid weeks of training that included role-plays, written and verbal tests, and a lot of classroom-based instruction on everything from what redlined terms we'd be willing to accept in our standard contract to the company's commitment to e-waste recycling. A real "drinking from the firehose" experience, the program gave me more information than I could retain, and a lot that I wouldn't need for quite some time.

I went home with a lot of facts but no real next step for advancing opportunities in my territory. So, when a recruiter called a month later to ask if I'd be open to interviewing for a more lucrative position, I took the call. I hadn't yet made much progress in my territory, and figured I really wouldn't be leaving much money on the table if I left this early in my tenure. I went to the interview, won the job, and left the Fortune 100 company, dropping it from my resume in short order. We both wasted a lot of time and energy in these few months of my ultimately abandoned job. The company spent a lot of money and resources on it, not to mention the opportunity costs of having no seller in seat during my recruitment, my few months of work, and the recruitment and onboarding of whoever filled the seat when I left.

A lot has changed in the intervening years, including the development of online sales enablement platforms that have permeated the business ecosystem. Today, my enablement teams have broken training into bite-sized learning modules that are delivered in a just-in-time fashion alongside homework assignments that actually advance their work in the field.

A new seller may consume a 15-minute video that tells them how to research their territory, and then spend the afternoon of their first day on the job using our CRM system to actually prioritize accounts based on this knowledge. After a few more training modules, they may then be launching their first email campaigns to low-risk prospects, and by the end of the week may be making their first cold calls to those prospects under the watch of a seasoned mentor. Training on contract terms and redlines won't come until much later in their onboarding, just before they actually need to put this knowledge to work with a real, live customer that's interested in signing an actual contract.

By orienting our onboarding into a "just-in-time" approach, we're still certifying sellers on all of the skills necessary to do the job but we're also giving them a fast start to succeeding in their territories, leading to more closed business. That's good for the seller and for the company.

Continuous Coaching

Advances in e-learning solutions, CRM system integrations, and AI have also made it possible for sellers to revisit these lessons just when they need them the most.

Learning is broken into small, easily-consumed chunks that can be re-presented to sellers again at just the moment they need to be used. As sellers progress deals in the CRM tool, it may present a reminder of the right MEDDPICCS question to ask in that specific stage or suggest the right case study or piece of collateral to present to an account in that industry for a deal of that size. AI tools that shadow live phone calls or online meetings may pop up cue cards to BDRs for how to respond to an objection that has just been raised, or a present reminder of the differentiation points against a competitor whose name has just been mentioned.

Aside from these in-the-moment coaching opportunities, my sales enablement teams also conduct a monthly analysis of our open opportunities through the lens of the sales methodology. By looking at which open opportunities have which MEDDPICCS questions answered, and which ones were problematic on the most recently-lost opportunities, they then identify themes for which skills need reinforcement at a company-wide level. Those themes can be addressed through monthly lunch-and-learn sessions or targeted team training.

You might use your call recording software to run ad-hoc mini-competitions to reinforce the learning in real time. So, for example, you might tell your teams that you're really working on getting better at introducing Joint Evaluation Plans with your customers over the next two weeks and ask each seller to submit a call recording of their best example of them having this conversation with a customer. The three sellers who submit the best examples across the company might win a small cash prize, and their recordings will be incorporated as "gold standard examples" in updated training materials on the topic.

CHAPTER 9

Quarterly Business Reviews

Following your annual kickoff, you should plan to have Quarterly Business Reviews (QBRs) that re-energize the team, report on results, and ensure that each seller is on track for great performance.

The earlier in the quarter they can be scheduled, the more likely they are to positively impact that quarter's sales performance. In practice, they involve a bit of data analysis of the immediately-concluded quarter. They also involve some self-reflection and preparation from individual sellers that you may not want as a distraction in the final selling weeks of the previous quarter. As a result, I've found they're best conducted in the second week of the first month of every quarter.

It is best to get these onto your team's calendar at the start of the year – for every quarter. The moving dates of Easter and many schools' Spring Break calendar may make it difficult for you to find an ideal Q2 QBR date if you operate on a calendar year. Americans will find that Q3's QBR is generally the week after they've been on Fourth of July holiday, so preparation time is tight.

Review Territory-Level Success Metrics

As I reach the end of a quarter, I convene my sales ops, marketing, and lead generation leaders to assess our progress against the annual plan, both booked revenue and created pipeline.

We review the Sales Velocity metrics from Chapter 3, at an aggregate level, and for each team. By doing this each quarter, we can look for trends that would indicate something is changing about our business environment. The introduction of a new competitor, a slowing of the overall economy, or change in the skill of our sellers might all manifest themselves as changes in one or more components of the Velocity calculation.

Similarly, I look to see whether the Velocity of a particular team is notably different from that of other teams. If so, this might indicate that they're operating in a unique market segment that needs to be treated differently than the rest or that there is something unique about the talent on that team or its leader that is important to recognize.

$$\frac{\# \times \$ \times \%}{L} = V$$

Opportunity Count | Deal Size | Win Rate

L = Length of Sales Cycle

V = Sales Velocity

Fig 9.1 Calculating Sales Velocity

For any metric performing worse than anticipated in the annual plan, determine what course-correcting actions can be taken in the coming quarters. Are there changes in marketing messages, or product pricing and packaging that can be considered? Is there a particular sales skill that can be refined to improve the win rate or reduce the length of the sales cycle? Each of these programs might be appropriate to roll out at your next QBR.

Also, conduct a territory-by-territory review of the Sales Velocity metrics to understand what is happening in each local region. Are there particular sellers who need skills training or upgrades? Are there geographies that are generating fewer opportunities or smaller deals than expected, and which could be helped by re-directing marketing spend or BDR resources? Determine course-correction plans for each of these where appropriate.

Build a QBR Agenda

Armed with these insights and course-correction plans, consider what else is happening at the organization that your team needs to know about. Are there products getting ready to launch? A new feature added to an existing offering? The integration of a newly-acquired company? Just like at sales kickoff, don't allocate time to it until you can articulate the action you want your team to take after the session, and how it will help the team to sell more going forward.

A lot of the topics that were introduced at kickoff also belong in the QBR. Report company-wide progress against plan for the prior quarter, identify and celebrate individuals who achieved their quarterly quota, recognize and give awards to team members who are doing things you'd like others to imitate, and revisit your annual theme to bring fresh vitality to the next 90-day sprint.

Conduct Team-Level QBRs with Individual Accountability

Alongside my all-hands QBR, my front-line managers conduct team-level QBRs where each seller presents progress on their own territory. Remembering that the optimal team size for any front-line manager is no more than eight sellers, the session can be conducted in three and a half hours, devoting twenty minutes per territory, with fifteen-minute breaks taken approximately every hour, and twenty minutes for the manager to reinforce major topics and themes at the beginning and end of the session:

0:00-0:10: Manager Overview to Team

0:10-0:30: Seller 1 Territory Review

0:30-0:50: Seller 2 Territory Review

0:50-1:10: Seller 3 Territory Review

1:10-1:25: Break

1:25-1:45: Seller 4 Territory Review

1:45-2:05: Seller 5 Territory Review

2:05-2:25: Seller 6 Territory Review

2:25-2:40: Break

2:40-3:00: Seller 7

3:00-3:20: Seller 8

3:20-3:30: Manager reviews themes, lessons learned, and next steps.

Get a Seller's QBR Template at

bit.ly/3ABkr1p

Within the 20-minute review, each seller presents to their peers the "state of the business" in their specific territory. It begins with a clear statement of their revenue production in the prior quarter compared to what they committed the prior quarter, and their assigned quota.

Next, the seller walks through a review of their actual Win Creation Waterfall metrics compared to the model, helping them to focus on which parts of the pipeline process they need to spend the most attention to in the coming quarter.

This discussion leads the seller into calling a Commitment, Best Case, and Forecast number for their territory in the quarter ahead using the definitions we'll describe in Chapter 10, with a brief summary of the individual deals they're working on to get there. This part of the review is brief, just a list of deal names, stages, and dollars. The full-blown discussion of what is happening in each deal and the strategy to win is saved for a Deal Clinic separate from the QBR.

Finally, the seller presents a three-question version of a SWOT analysis: What's going well? What's not going well? What can I control and experiment with in the coming quarter? For the third question, I emphasize that it should be a discussion about what the sellers themselves can do to achieve a different outcome. Many under-performing sellers come to QBRs ready to blame others for their failures. Their discussion of "what's not going well" may include arguments such as a need to be paired with a better BDR, or that they require more inbound marketing leads, or any number of other items that are outside the seller's control.

While those may be valid in the territory, and the manager does need a mechanism to collect them, determine if they're actionable, and do something about them, the QBR is about focusing the seller on developing a plan that is in their control to execute for the coming quarter. So, the final question redirects their energy to making a commitment about how their own actions will change in the next months with the hope that they'll show up in the "what's going well" segment of next quarter's QBR. If time allows, an expanded version of the territory review might be co-presented with the solutions engineer or BDR that is paired with the seller. They might share their lead generation plan for the coming months, observations about industry, buying trends they're seeing in their accounts, or updates on other collaborative projects.

The manager should take notes in each of these sessions, and summarize key themes and action items after the last seller has presented. It is likely that many sellers will be struggling with the same issues and roadblocks, and the manager's wrap-up is a great place to brainstorm ways that they can work together as a team to address them.

Summarize Across Teams

A week after the teams have conducted their QBRs, I like to get my front line managers together to review major themes they observed. A virtual meeting is fine for this, but should allow opportunities for each manager to present major takeaways of what's working and what's not in their team, as well as provide some brainstorming time to discuss what asks you have of the larger organization, or what cross-team initiatives might be undertaken as a result of what was learned.

The manager should be having the quarterly Performance Improvement Plan conversations from Chapter 8 with their sellers right around the time of the QBR meeting. This may also be a good time, then, for the manager to update their Talent Nine Block from Chapter 5, and share any key insights with me and our HR business partner so that we can monitor appropriate followup.

CHAPTER 10

Forecasting

I had an opportunity to be a guest on a popular sales podcast, and we got to talking about the troubling fact that the average tenure of sales leaders is about 18 months. These leaders are expensive to recruit and expensive to pay, so we asked if we are really giving up on them simply because they couldn't completely change the sales outcomes in their first year on the job. I believe that most sales leaders aren't getting fired for missing their numbers, it's because they couldn't forecast accurately. The host agreed, saying that his mentor always told him that, "Missing your number is bad, but missing your forecast is death."

In Chapter 1, we talked about how the assumptions you put in your annual plan largely determine whether you will meet or miss your number for the year. In this way, it is the single most important thing you will do as a CRO to lead to strong performance. As you start working against that plan, the effort you put into creating a consistent, reliable cadence through which you can set everyone's expectations around that performance is the single most important thing you will do to ensure you continue to be a CRO.

Four Numbers

When I talk about forecasting, I mean "predicting how much revenue will come into the business over a given period of time." That period is generally the current month, the current quarter, and the entire year.

For each of these timeframes, I actually like to identify four different numbers: Pipeline, Commit, Best Case, and Forecast, and get everyone in the organization aligned on their definitions.

Pipeline is the most straightforward number to report. It represents the sum total of every opportunity you have in your CRM system that has a close date within the time period. Recognizing that most SaaS teams have a win rate of between 25% and 35%, a forecast report that shows less than 3-4 times quota coverage raises concerns amongst the board and leadership team.

Commit is the number you absolutely know will be delivered from your pipeline without a doubt. It's the "take it to the bank" number that you can promise your CFO and investors as the absolute worst-case scenario – and it's the one to run your business on if you're extremely conservative. Commitments are usually made up of specifically named deals, but if one of those deals doesn't close, you know that you can replace it with another one to deliver the committed revenue in the timeframe expected. Highly transactional businesses that create and close deals in small time horizons may also not be able to name the specific deals in their commitment, but they can use historical run-rate performance as a place to get to a reasonable commitment.

Best Case is the "best of all possible worlds" number. It is generally the collection of every deal you have any likelihood of closing within the given time frame. It's perhaps not your entire pipeline (you may be tracking some deals that you know you're going to lose but still leave open in your CRM system for various reasons), but it's pretty close. Communicating a best case places an upper limit expectation of performance, but "all the stars would have to align perfectly in every deal" to achieve it.

Forecast, then, falls somewhere between Commit and Best Case. It's a reasonable assumption, given the imperfect data you may have at any point in time, and is likely to change as the quarter progresses and you resolve unknowns in your deals.

Most businesses like to build their plans around Forecast instead of Commit, as the goldilocks-inspired "not too large and not too small" nature of the forecast number shouldn't leave them with too much risk to mitigate if you underperform expectations or too much lost investment opportunity when you wildly overperform. While reporting Pipeline, Commit, and Best Case are largely "science," Forecast is the part of the process that requires a bit more art.

Three Forecasting Methods

CROs who forecast in a black box, just providing a number that they subsequently miss, have the shortest tenures. Their boards and colleagues know they can't trust the forecast for important decisions and have no idea how to adjust expectations around the number they're given.

Knowing that most businesses will find the Commit too conservative and want to plan expenses and investments based on a Forecast number, I like to "show my work" to anyone making decisions based on my reported number. In this way, I'm spreading responsibility around with others as we make the most important decisions about our business's cash flow. That work is usually achieved by calculating the Forecast in three different ways, which hopefully produce answers that largely agree with one another.

Stage Weighting

Often, past performance is the best predictor of future performance. So, one method to forecast a month or quarter's worth of business begins with looking at your current open pipeline and identifying how many dollars and deals are in each stage. Then, you can look back to historical data about the percentage of dollars or deals from each stage that closed in the relevant month/quarter and apply that trend to your current pipeline to arrive at a forecast number.

For example, Figure 10.1 shows a company with $15.4M worth of opportunities in its pipeline at the beginning of the quarter. Looking at how much pipeline they had in each stage at the start of their prior four quarters and what was won within each quarter, they have an average 2% win rate in-quarter on Stage 1 opportunities, 95% on Stage 6, and a variety in between. Applying those win rates to the makeup of the current-quarter pipeline by stage, a stage weighting approach forecasts a $1.8M finish.

	Average Win Rate Prior 4 Quarters	Current Dollars in Pipeline	Forecast
Stage 1	2%	$ 6,382,059.00	$ 127,641.18
Stage 2	3%	$ 4,204,817.00	$ 126,144.51
Stage 3	5%	$ 2,836,780.00	$ 141,839.00
Stage 4	21%	$ 337,912.00	$ 70,961.52
Stage 5	63%	$ 723,901.00	$ 456,057.63
Stage 6	95%	$ 938,175.00	$ 891,266.25
		$ 15,423,644.00	$1,813,910.09

Fig 10.1: Calculating a Stage-Weighted Forecast

This method works well for companies with stable businesses and consistent performance. However, a number of issues can make it inaccurate.

First, stage weighting assumes that win rates are consistent by stage in the prior four quarters and that the average will also be relevant in this quarter. However, there may be situations where seasonality changes the win rate, including much higher win rates in the last quarter of the year or much lower win rates during the summer months. In these cases, the average of the prior four quarters may not result in an accurate forecast.

Get a Stage Weighting Calculator at

bit.ly/3MjU9Df

Similarly, there may be factors in your business that are changing today's win rate for better or worse. Perhaps you've launched a skills training plan or upgraded the talent on your team so that win rates are improving each quarter. Maybe a competitor has recently introduced a new product, making it much harder to win. In these instances, it may make sense to look at the win rate trends and try to extrapolate a per-stage win rate to use for this quarter that accounts for them.

A final challenge with the stage weighting method is that it assumes that the deals you have within each stage today are largely the same size and match the average deal size of those of the prior quarters you're using in your model. That's not always the case. In Figure 10.1's example, there may be a single opportunity in Stage 5 that is valued at $723k. This model weighs a 63% win rate to forecast $456k to close. Yet the outcome of this deal is going to be binary; it will either be won or lost. That means it will either contribute $0 or $723k to the forecast, barring a little bit of discounting that may be needed to get the deal done. The "lumpier" a pipeline is within its stages, the less accurate the stage-weighting approach is going to be.

Seller Rollup

Another approach to forecasting accounts for this variability by putting specific, named opportunities in or out of the forecast based on personal judgment. For each deal in the pipeline, I ask sellers to flag them in our CRM system as either "committed" for the quarter, a "best case or stretch" for the quarter, or a "pipeline deal" that is not expected to be won in the quarter.

Sellers often do not assign these categories accurately and tend to change them weekly. I had a seller who loved to feel like a hero who saved the day at the end of a difficult quarter, so began each quarter with few-to-no deals committed. He then showed up with signed customer contracts in the final weeks of the quarter when the pressure on the team was getting high. Another seller always committed a half-dozen deals each quarter, only to see each one dropping out of their forecast in the final three weeks with the explanation that "the customer broke our heart with some surprising bad news – but we can commit this next half dozen deals next quarter."

I mitigate these very human issues by asking my front line managers to run a series of Deal Clinics to inspect opportunities more closely, and then track a "manager commitment category," using that commit/best/pipeline designation for our forecast. I have our CRM security set so that sellers don't see what their managers have committed (or not) to let them have great development conversations about how the seller forecasted the deal and why it did or didn't happen as planned.

Because my managers are more senior, forecasts based on their commitments are better than those based on seller commitments. Allowing managers to forecast a dollar amount by deal helps even further, allowing them to say, "I know this seller has it in CRM as a $450k deal, but also know we'll have to offer another 10% discount to get it done, so I'm forecasting it at $405k." While manager forecasts are better than front-line sellers, they're subject to human error, too.

While I wouldn't feel comfortable running my entire business based on a roll-up forecasting process, I incorporate it because it drives deal-level conversations through all levels of the organization—from front-line sellers to me and the rest of the executive leadership team—and it builds the skills of everyone involved to better understand how our deals actually work.

Revenue Operations Tools

In recent years, revenue operations tools have been able to incorporate AI-assisted analytics of both the structured CRM data and unstructured email, call transcript, and other data from prospect interactions to arrive at very accurate forecast numbers. The approach is similar to the stage weighting method but uses a lot more data dimensions than deal size and stage to ask of every deal in the pipeline, "Where have we seen deals like this in the past, and what was their outcome?"

The results include the idiosyncrasies of the specific seller involved in the deal and their historic behaviors, like the number of times close dates change, the typical size of the change, whether the close came earlier or later, and whether the final deal amount ultimately came in higher or lower than the originally forecast number. These tools also take into account things like the historical results of working with prospects of a similar size in a similar industry, with a similar number of meetings with similar decision-makers.

The landscape of these vendors continues to evolve, and the variety and success of AI offerings are moving so quickly that almost any recommendation would be outdated by the time this book has gone to print. However, there are great ones out there. My currently preferred tool has been able to predict how my quarter ends with 98% accuracy by the second week of the quarter. It's done so for 17 out of 18 quarters - missing that mark only when the COVID pandemic shut down businesses during the final three weeks of our quarter.

The Forecasting Cadence

Each of these forecasting methodologies has its strengths and weaknesses, so I like to use all three to manage my business. When the three numbers are very close to one another, I have a very high degree of confidence in them. When one method produces a very different result than the others, it suggests that something non-standard is happening, and we need to spend time diagnosing why before settling on which number we're most confident moving forward with.

I like to provide a weekly forecast update to my executive team colleagues and my board, and use the following cadence to make that happen:

MONDAY: Front line managers conduct one-on-one meetings with sellers, ensuring the CRM system is updated with their best estimated Close Date, Revenue Amount, Deal Stage, and Forecast Category (commit/best case/pipeline) by the end of the day.

TUESDAY: Managers update the CRM with their own Forecast Category, while revenue operations runs an updated Stage Weighted Forecast based on current data.

WEDNESDAY: Front line managers attend a forecasting call with me, revenue operations, and representatives from other departments in the organization. They provide a narrative around the committed and best-case opportunities, paying particular attention to any requests they need from the rest of the company that could move any from best-case to committed. While a formal Deal Desk process runs every day of the week to review requests for non-standard contract terms or unusual discounts, this venue creates a space for finance, product management, marketing, and implementation teams to identify overarching themes across opportunities that might influence their own work.

THURSDAY: A Go-to-Market Flash Report is emailed to all stakeholders, including sales leaders, the executive team, finance leaders, and the board. It provides week-by-week updates on how the pipeline and bookings have progressed, compares it to trends and expectations, and surfaces a qualitative narrative that explains the reported data.

Throughout the week, front line managers hold Deal Clinics to help diagnose what is happening in opportunities and coach sellers in ways to improve our likelihood of winning.

The Go-to-Market Flash Report

As CRO, I'm constantly asked for my best understanding of our forecast from a wide range of people.

My CEO, CFO, and executive team want to know if we're on track against our commitments to the board. The board wants to know if we need to trim costs to adjust for a revenue shortfall or are anticipating a surplus of dollars through overperformance that can be allocated to additional hires, product developments, or other investments in the business. The implementation team wants to start planning the volume of work that will be handed to them soon, and so on.

Producing a weekly Flash Report creates an easy answer to all these questions and ensures the data is fairly fresh. Decisions made from it are never based on an understanding of the business that is more than a week old. The highlight of the Flash Report is a single graphic that shows a week-by-week progression of a few key metrics in our business:

- The cumulative revenue that has been booked in the quarter for each week that has passed

- The total revenue we forecast to close in that quarter and how that forecast has moved in each week that has passed

- The total revenue our business plan calls for us to close in that quarter

- The total Quota on the Street based on our current sales headcount (and their stage in the onboarding/ramping process) for each week that has passed

These data are presented against the backdrop of how the immediately preceding quarter played out and how the same quarter in the prior year unfolded for additional insight into whether or not we will achieve our objective.

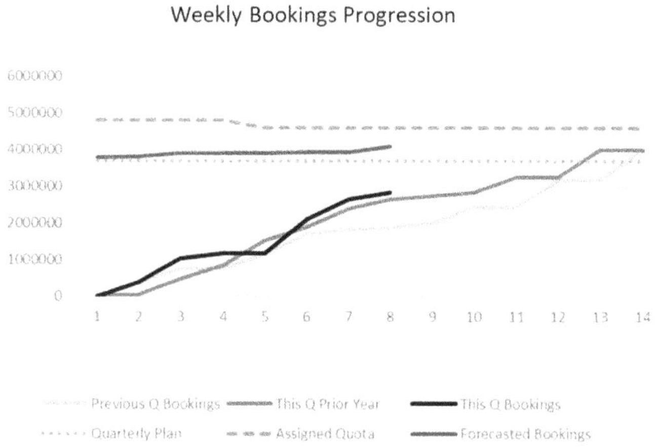

Fig 10.2: Bookings Analysis for the Weekly Flash Report

In Figure 10.2, we have just completed the eighth week of the quarter. We've already booked $2.8M of revenue, which is ahead of the $1.8M booked by the eighth week of the prior quarter and the $2.6M booked at this point in the same quarter of last year. The forecast has steadily increased over the past few weeks and now anticipates $4.1M of bookings. That is well ahead of the $3.7M called for in the plan for the quarter but still below the assigned quota on the street, even after the departure of a seller in Week 5. This is a positive update!

Alongside this chart, a brief narrative may identify whether there is a big disparity between a stage-weighted, roll-up, or rev ops tool's forecast and what they each are. It might also provide an explanation for the Week 5 staffing change (voluntary or involuntary termination, reasons why) and perhaps a few brief highlights on the progression of critical deals. It should not, however, provide an exhaustive list of every deal in the pipeline, which is an inappropriate level of detail for the board and many on the distribution list.

Accompanying the chart should be a brief table highlighting performance and forecast by team:

Sales Team	Quota		Forecast			Bookings	Gap to Plan				Pipeline Coverage To Forecast	
	Quarterly Plan	Assigned Quota	Manager Commit	Manager Best Case	Manager Forecast	QTD Bookings	Bookings to Plan	Forecast to Plan	Commit To Plan	Best Case to Plan	Open Pipeline	Pipeline Ratio
Sr. New Logo	$ 1,665,000	$ 2,158,000	$ 1,415,832	$ 2,186,482	$ 1,640,154	$ 928,471	$ (736,529)	$ (24,846)	$ (249,168)	$ 521,482	$ 2,063,880	2.9
Jr New Logo	$ 925,000	$ 1,110,000	$ 974,183	$ 1,310,481	$ 1,025,096	$ 775,210	$ (149,790)	$ 100,096	$ 49,183	$ 385,481	$ 799,635	3.2
Install Base	$ 1,110,000	$ 1,332,000	$ 1,225,719	$ 1,618,920	$ 1,435,134	$ 1,125,800	$ 15,800	$ 325,134	$ 115,719	$ 508,920	$ 1,082,670	3.5
All Team Sales	$ 3,700,000	$ 4,600,000	$ 3,615,734	$ 5,115,883	$ 4,100,384	$ 2,829,481	$ (870,519)	$ 400,384	$ (84,266)	$ 1,415,883	$ 3,946,185	3.1
			98%	138%	111%	76%						

Fig 10.3: Performance and Forecasting Details by Team

Finally, the flash report should provide some guidance on confidence for future quarters by including an update on pipeline development alongside any narrative about key campaigns in progress, notable new deals added to the pipeline, or other brief commentaries. A weekly pipeline progress report takes a similar form as the weekly bookings chart, mapping the cumulative pipeline created week by week against the progress of the prior quarter and the same quarter in prior years.

In this example, the pipeline called for in the annual plan and the BDR capacity are mapped with monthly stairsteps, recognizing that this team is managed to monthly development goals instead of weekly ones.

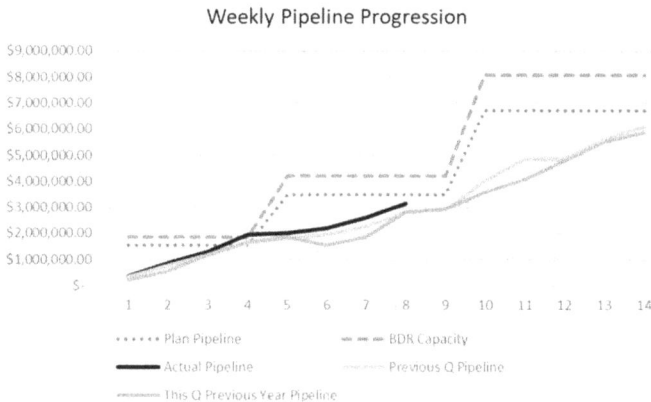

Fig 10.4: Pipeline Analysis for the Weekly Flash Report

By providing clear and concise updates on your forecasts, you establish yourself as a CRO who deeply understands the business's performance and the factors that will shape its future. This communication fosters trust with the leadership and investor teams, allowing for more strategic conversations focused on future actions rather than simply trying to agree on the present state.

That's the kind of CRO you want to be.

CHAPTER 11
Skills Coaching for Sellers

In many organizations, individuals are promoted to sales leadership because they are high-performing individual contributors. Many of them fall into the trap of thinking of themselves as super-sellers, who now have a team of eight direct reports who source deals that they will now come into and close. Such leaders have limited future potential because there is an upper limit to how many deals they can work in a day, and they quickly find the outer limits of their personal reach.

One day, I asked my physician father how he learned to do surgeries, and he explained that the medical profession has a "watch one, do one, teach one" mentality. I suspect that the training was a bit more extensive than that—even in the 1970s when he was going through school—but it's a framework that I think works really well.

Watching someone perform the sales skill well gives a seller some exposure to "what good looks like." Doing the skill while a manager or other trusted colleague is close enough to jump in and take over if things go really poorly creates a safe way for sellers to refine their craft. Teaching someone else how to do it forces the seller to think about each of the nuanced details that ensure success and mastery of the skill at hand.

With this in mind, I encourage managers to get in the field with sellers as often as possible but to resist the temptation to jump in and take over the deal on their own at the first sign of struggle. Yes, it might mean that a deal requires an extra meeting to close, or a negotiation will result in a little bit more of a discount than ideal, but letting a seller make a mistake and then recover from it can really cement key learnings.

This process is what an ex-military leader of mine once described as "Letting them make the mistakes that might result in losing a finger, stepping in on those that will cause them to lose an arm." Finding exactly where on that spectrum to intervene is an art. We might want to refine the metaphor to just be "creating superficial flesh wounds," but it's a process that works.

While many of the best learnings come from in-the-field coaching by the manager, leaders quickly run out of hours in the day to participate in all the deals they'd like, even if they've kept to the "no more than eight direct reports" rule of organizational design. The Deal Clinic process creates a more scalable way to get sellers coached on all their opportunities from their manager and others without investing their time in attending every sales meeting.

A Conversation Rooted In Methodology

Sellers are a social bunch and can easily spend an hour talking about a given opportunity in their pipeline. Details like where the decision maker went to school, what they had for lunch in the last meeting, and a word-for-word replay of the last sales call can easily consume our time without advancing the deal in any measurable way.

For a Deal Clinic, then, I like to structure a conversation around the nine MEDDPICCS questions our methodology says every deal needs to have answered to get to a win.

The tempo of the clinic is fast. Like a doctor conducting an annual physical exam, a leader running a Deal Clinic should be able to get through the major issues in about fifteen minutes. Run down the nine questions and determine if we have an answer to them, whether the

Get a Deal Clinic
Template at

bit.ly/4dC8cAa

answer is one we like, and what we can do to steer them in a better direction. Finish the Deal Clinic by reviewing the Joint Evaluation Plan, adding steps and activities to help fill in the gaps on the deal, and plan to run another checkup clinic when the next major steps have happened.

A Deal Clinic shouldn't take a lot of time for a seller to prepare for. Ideally, the nine process questions are represented as text fields on the opportunity in your CRM system, and your sellers update them in real-time as they engage with their prospects.

Rather than putting together a big PowerPoint deck to prepare for a Clinic, sellers should be able to pull up the opportunity screen in CRM and use it to guide the conversation, taking notes and updating the JEP as they go along.

Deal Clinic Attendees

If your organization has invested in a sales enablement team, they should be responsible for scheduling Deal Clinics and facilitating the conversations so they stay on track and on time. Their experience across the breadth of clinics can help identify major training needs and respond programmatically.

My best enablement teams have given me insights like "the most common challenge raised in all of our Deal Clinics last month has been in connecting with the executive sponsor," leading us to then launch a mini-training on the subject the following month alongside a competition that gave prizes to the sellers who put the training to use most effectively in recorded sales calls.

In many organizations with smaller enablement investments, a seller's front line manager needs to be a meeting facilitator and timekeeper. They almost always should be the primary coach. As often as possible, I like to include uninvolved third parties, too. Managers who aren't in the direct reporting line for the given seller or deal can give great dispassionate advice that isn't influenced by a personal interest in whether the deal is ultimately won or lost or by having firsthand experiences with the prospect.

It's helpful for me as a CRO to attend Deal Clinics to get insight into the broad trends of what's happening with my organization. However, there wouldn't be enough hours in the day to attend every Clinic, and sellers often get nervous or feel overly scrutinized when a member of the c-suite comes to their reviews. Other sellers are great participants in Deal Clinics. Since a single review can go quickly, I like to group a few of them together into an hour-long session, where different deals from different sellers are all examined. Each of those sellers should listen to and actively participate in all of the other clinics in the session, not just show up for their own fifteen-minute spot.

Hearing one seller get coaching on an opportunity can often create that "watch one" component of learning that my dad talked about. Since many issues are the same from deal to deal, coaching can also be more efficient in the second and third reviews, where we recognize, "This is the same thing we just talked about in the first opportunity, and you can try the same thing here." By encouraging sellers to share their own experiences and make suggestions to others, we're also often able to get that "teach one" level of mastery that Dad's training approach uses.

If your organization has solutions engineers, they should also be included in each of the Clinics for opportunities they are working on. Professionals from outside the go-to-market organization should be occasional participants. Hearing deal-level information can help guide marketing, product management, and others in understanding the trends that might shape their business.

Deal Clinic Timing

Because they're so quick to execute and are the most effective development tool I have outside of in-the-field coaching, the Deal Clinic is an integral part of my weekly operating cadence. Front line managers should be holding Deal Clinics at least once a week and should be finding a cadence to make sure that every deal has a Clinic on a timeframe that can improve our odds of winning it.

In practice, this has meant that we create some programmatic rules in our CRM system to flag that it's time for a Clinic to happen. This is always tied to achieving a specific stage, often with a trigger like, "Once a deal is in Stage 3, it is real enough that it's worth us looking at it more closely." Opportunities that linger too long in a given stage also get identified for Deal Clinics. My sales operations team can provide benchmarks on the average length of time any of our won deals were spent in each of our sales stages. A weekly report of active opportunities that have been stuck in a stage longer than the average becomes the starting point for next week's list of Deal Clinics to hold.

Sellers often nominate their own deals for a quick Clinic whenever they feel it'd be beneficial for another set of eyes to look at their opportunities. We also often proactively schedule a follow-up Clinic any time we've conducted one that has a long list of action items, choosing a date to check in on progress against the tasks and impact they've had.

CHAPTER 12

Interacting With Your Board

I mentioned in Chapter 10 that the average tenure of a sales leader is about a year and a half. Many professionals believe this high turnover rate is because the teams they led don't hit revenue expectations. Yet, in Chapter 1, we learned that 91% of teams don't hit their annual target. While I think there is some merit in a narrative that says a new leader is hired to hit a goal, they miss it in their first year, and the board spends another six months recruiting a replacement that takes over when the first leader is hitting their 18-month anniversary. It sounds logical, but I just don't think that CROs are getting fired for missing quota as much as they are for miscommunicating expectations with their leadership and investor teams.

Get a Flash Report Template at

bit.ly/3WZu4yj

In my sales career, I've generally survived long past this 18-month average time in the seat. And yet, I've had many difficult conversations with boards where I tell them that we're going to miss our monthly target or that we're unlikely to achieve the target for six more months.

And while nobody liked hearing that news from me, they appreciated that I could also explain what was going wrong in the business, what we were doing to correct it, and how long it would take before we'd get to a different outcome. My boards had confidence in my predictions, saw measurable, quantifiable progress towards improvement every month to further solidify their faith in me, and ultimately celebrated when we finally achieved a possibly revised plan at some point down the line.

I think that's the real distinction between CROs who are replaced quickly and those who have long careers. Nobody expects that your team will be perfect or that you're going to always achieve your number, and I'm actually really skeptical of leaders whose resumes say they've never missed plan. What is expected is that the CRO accurately understands what is going to happen, understands why it is going to happen, and gives their boards an opportunity to course-correct the overall strategy as early as possible.

That's why "great board communication" is a key part of the CRO's job description. It's human nature to dislike giving bad news, and many CROs avoid interacting with their investors when times are tough. I embrace board communication, though – on a weekly, monthly, and quarterly basis, in good times and in bad – which is what I believe has led to my long-tenured success.

A Cadence of Written Communication

A lot of the communication with the board is built from the data-driven reports already discussed in this book. Every week, my board should expect to get a flash report emailed to them with the quick-to-digest charts of weekly bookings and pipeline progression detailed in Chapter 10.

Monthly, I also like to share a one-page dashboard of metrics that show our pipeline, bookings, and forecast against the monthly, quarterly, and annual plan. I also include a brief summary of key initiatives and highlight areas of the report that are underperforming against plan.

Monthly Booked Revenue

Actual vs. Plan	1.646M vs 1.470M	112%
Actual vs Same Month Prior Year	1.646M vs 1.358M	121%

Year to Date Booked Revenue

Actual vs. Plan	7.892M vs 7.692M	103%
Actual vs. Prior Year	7.892M vs 7.358M	107%

Quarterly Bookings Forecast

Forecast vs. Plan	4.100M vs 3.700M	111%
Forecast vs. Prior Year	4.100M vs 3.318M	124%

Annual Bookings Forecast

Full Year Forecast vs. Plan	15.985M vs. 16.125M	99%
Full Year Forecast vs. Prior Year	15.985M vs 14.892M	107%

Quarterly Pipeline Health

Open Pipeline To Reach Forecast	3.946M vs. 1.270M	303%
Open Pipeline to Reach Plan	3.946M vs. .870M	454%

Staffing Health

Assigned Quota vs. Plan	4,600 vs 3,700	124%
Number of Sellers Vs. Plan	19 vs 20	95%

Other Intiatives

Status of Onboarding Redesign	85% complete
Status of Messaging Re-write	100% complete
Status of Product Pricing Intiative	25% complete

Fig 12.1: A Monthly Report of Key Metrics

167

In this example, the company has had a great month, booking 112% of its monthly plan, 21% better than the same month in the prior year. This reflects an annual trend that shows it's performing at 103% of plan for the full year so far, 7% better than where it was at this point in the prior year.

They're similarly forecast to have a strong finish to the quarter, expecting to reach 111% of the quarterly plan for a 24% improvement over the same quarter in the prior year. They've got pipeline coverage of 4.54 times what they still need to book to hit the quarterly plan and 3.03 times what they need to hit the forecast they're calling. On a full-year basis, a slowdown in future quarters is anticipated. They're forecasting a $140k miss against the full-year plan and a finish that is 7% better than the prior year.

On the right side of the report, we see some qualitative updates. They're one seller short of what the plan called for, though they still have an assigned quota on the street that is 24% higher than the total bookings plan. They've finished a project to rewrite their company message and are close to finishing the redesign of their onboarding programs. Still, they're just starting work on an initiative to modify prices on their product packages.

Structured Verbal Communication

When the board meets in person, I include the latest updates to each of these charts. They don't require much discussion because the board has already seen the data repeatedly. Instead, I spend the majority of my time talking to a few additional slides that provide qualitative updates on "what we're doing about what we see in these data."

In this hypothetical report, we're showing overperformance year to date against our bookings target but are expected to lose all of those gains and fall a bit short of the overall bookings number by the end of the year. My board slides would include some discussion about why that is expected to happen with accompanying data. Maybe the fact that we're one headcount down against the plan is the earliest sign of an exodus we know is underway as sellers flock to another employer who pays much higher salaries, or perhaps we expect our competitor to launch a product that is going to significantly lower our win rates for the remainder of the year.

Whatever the story, the final slides of my board deck would identify my planned response, alongside any additional requests we might have in strategy or spending (like the revision of our comp plans or additional marketing effort to launch a competitive takeout campaign). The result is that my board and I spend less time trying to forecast the weather and a lot more time aligning on the strategy we'll pursue to respond to it.

Ad-hoc Communication

Most private equity companies I've worked for have also had a board member or two who are functional specialists in go-to-market issues. As an operating advisor, I also work for PE companies to provide this sort of go-to-market mentorship and consulting for the companies in their portfolio.

These are relationships that you should use to your advantage. Many junior CROs fear sharing too much with their board or advisors, particularly if it's bad news. And yet, the PE firm has invested in these people specifically because they've been in your shoes and experienced the good and bad times you're facing. Rather than judging your performance negatively, they can advise on what's worked (or not) for them in the past – helping you speed through difficulties.

At the end of the day, all of these people are investors in your company. They succeed when you succeed, so it's in their interest to stick with you through the bad times and help you come out the other end a better company for it.

Cross-Portfolio Talent Development

A discussion of board communication wouldn't be complete without also thinking about the kinds of conversations you can engage in that aren't part of the "official, formal board process."

Most PE firms I've worked with have created networks that connect the go-to-market leaders of each of their portfolio companies with one another. The networks may be informal chat groups, videoconference meetings periodically, or in-person annual get-togethers. Regardless of the format, they're done to connect you with others in your role who may face similar challenges and who could learn from your shared experiences. Don't overlook these "optional" events.

PE firms also often extend these programs to your next line of leadership. Recognizing that they're always going to be buying new companies that might need great sales leaders, they may certainly tap you for a new role when you're finished at your current business. They may also know that you've got a great VP who is ready to take the next step in their career, turning to them to fill an opening in the portfolio with someone "in the family."

Even when my direct reports aren't included in portfolio-wide development meetings, I like to bring them to observe my own board meetings so that they can start to understand the kinds of issues and topics that they'll need to wrestle with when they take a CRO position of their own.

CHAPTER 13

Managing Renewals and Price Increases

As a head of sales, it's easy to focus on the new logo motion as your primary measure of success. But for SaaS companies valued based on their Annual Recurring Revenue, the factor that will most influence your success is what you do with your existing customer base.

Take, for example, a company with $100M in ARR. This means that in a given calendar year, their customers spend $100M on their products. They'll have to pay $100M again to continue using them for another year, making it "recurring revenue." A CRO might be recruited to the organization and given the mission of "growing ARR 20%." Their goal, then, would be to start the next year with $120M in recurring revenue. On the surface, the new CRO might believe they need to sell $20M of new contracts in the year to achieve that goal.

Yet, movement within the existing customer base can significantly change that target. Some customers will go out of business and not renew their contracts. Others may not renew because they don't like your product or decide to switch to a competitor. When we measure the percentage of recurring revenue that the company retains from existing companies over a year, we are calculating its "Gross Retention" rate. For example, if our hypothetical company only renewed $80M of its initial $100M of ARR, it would have a gross retention rate of 80%. That CRO trying to finish the year with $120M of ARR will have to find $40M of new business, not $20M.

Helping out, some customers will expand their usage of the product. When the economy is good, customers may hire more employees and place orders for additional licenses to your product without any sales motion at all. They may acquire a new company that they want to have using your product, or your team may proactively sell additional modules or solutions to your install base. It's possible that growth in your accounts more than offsets any of the losses so that the same customer base that spent $100M last year now spends $104M this year. This calculation is called "net retention" and would be 104% in our example, leaving just $16M of new business to be found for our new CRO.

A healthy gross retention rate for a SaaS company is anything higher than 90%, and anything higher than 95% is considered excellent. Healthy SaaS companies should have net retention rates over 105%, while the best in the industry may hit over 135%. Due to the impact these factors can have on your overall success, a CRO must have a well-managed plan to maximize the net retention of their customer base.

Contractual Terms

A solid retention plan begins with the language in your customer contracts. Great software companies build customer contracts that minimize the effort and maximize the likelihood of high retention rates:

Multi-year Contracts

Winning a new logo customer takes a lot of time and effort. Ideally, you don't expend that same effort with them every year to secure the renewal. That's why it's common practice for SaaS companies to sell contracts with multi-year terms, often three to five-year commitments. If all of your customers are on three-year contracts, it means that you'll only have to work with about a third of them each year to secure the renewal, while companies that sell only one-year contracts have to re-contract every customer in their install base every year.

One company I worked for calculated that they actually spent about $1.07 to win and implement a customer worth $1 of ARR. However, the multi-year contract and low cost of effort to maintain the relationship meant that it only cost them 10¢ to maintain the revenue for the second and third years—meaning that they were enjoying pure profit from the customer after 14 months of working together.

Automatic Renewals

When the initial contract term is completed, a best practice in SaaS is for the contract to automatically renew for an additional term unless the customer expressly cancels it. Ideally, a three-year contract automatically renews for an additional three years, although this may be negotiated down to automatic one-year renewals after the initial term.

Pre-negotiated Price Increases

To win the initial deal, you may have discounted from your list price for the products purchased. Contract terms that dictate that the discount only applies for the first year of a three-year term or that automatic renewals will revert to the un-discounted price work to your advantage. Expect customers to negotiate a cap on annual price increases, often choosing a flat percentage (say 3% or 5%), a published Consumer Price Index, or a combination of the two (no more than CPI plus 2%).

Depending on the economic environment and the strength of the negotiation team, it may be in your best interest to remain silent in the contract about the price increase, betting that your solution will become so entrenched in the customer organization and create such a high return on investment that almost any price increase will stick.

I once worked at a company that showed customers a list price of $500 per user per year and discounted it 50% to $250 in the initial term, only to raise the price back to $500 (and then $550, and then $600) in subsequent renewals without any complaints because the customer calculated the ROI for the solution itself was over $10,000 per user.

Cancellation Process and Timing

Creating a process that makes it harder for customers to cancel can also help with net retention rates. Your contract terms may stipulate that a contract can only be canceled by the customer in writing, and it must be received no later than 90 days prior to its renewal. Customers may forget their contract was up for renewal until they receive the invoice for the next year. If your finance team doesn't send those invoices out until 45 days prior to the new term starting, these customers may be locked into your solution for at least another year. Even if they immediately send a cancellation notice that is effective at the end of that year, you've bought yourself 12 months to figure out why they're unhappy, do something about it, and negotiate a new contract to continue the relationship.

User Count Mechanics

A lot of SaaS software is sold on a "per user, per year" basis. While most solutions have a mechanism in place to count the number of active users, few software companies or clients pay active attention to it. The best-run companies give their customers the ability to request new users any time they'd like or even have an automated system in place where the solution synchronizes with the customer's HR system to create user licenses for newly hired employees and decommission licenses for recently departed ones.

In practice, this means that total user count fluctuates throughout the year as the customer's employee population grows and shrinks—maybe it's 403 users one month, and then it's 398 the next. Perhaps there's seasonality to their business that sees the employee count rise as high as 440 in the summer, but settle back down around 400 at the end of the year.

SaaS companies that only check the user count once a year at the time of the renewal may miss out on the serious revenue that these fluctuations can produce. Including contract terms stipulating user counts will be taken and invoiced quarterly, monthly, weekly, or even daily can provide incremental revenue effortlessly.

Some companies take this even further, stipulating "high water mark" language that says total user counts only adjust upwards, not down. Once our hypothetical customer has been billed for 440 users, they will continue to renew 440 users even if the total need at the time has fallen to 398. At some point, customers will grow frustrated with this term and threaten to cancel their contract if it's not re-negotiated. Still, it may add notable incremental revenue for a large number of customers for many years.

Proactively Working The Renewals Plan

In Chapter 1, we discussed creating an annual plan that starts by understanding which customers are up for renewal, what their contract allows for in that renewal, and what their satisfaction level is. Based on what we think is possible, we set a customer-by-customer strategy for how we'd like each renewal to proceed.

Customer	Current ARR	Increase Allowed	Satisfaction	Multi-Year	Renewal Date	STRATEGY
Apex Zenith Group	$ 44,516.00	2% YELLOW	NO	Jan	Multi-year with 0%
NovaWave	$276,430.00	GREEN	NO	Feb	Multi-year with 2%
Stellar Synergy	$ 15,796.00	2% GREEN	YES	Feb	2%
LuminaCore	$589,478.00	6% GREEN	YES	Mar	6%
Quantum Innovations	$138,574.00	0% GREEN	YES	Mar	0%
Veridian	$310,176.00	2% RED	YES	Apr	Churn
Ethos	$115,239.00	GREEN	YES	Apr	5%
TerraForge	$568,656.00	YELLOW	YES	May	Multi-year with 0%
Chronosync Tech	$216,118.00	7% YELLOW	YES	May	3.50%

Fig 13.1: Translating Customer Health and Renewal Terms into a Monthly Renewal Strategy

As each month progresses, we want to have a meeting with our renewals team, our customer success managers, and our executive team to determine how we can exceed that plan. In this example, we assumed that Veridian was so unhappy that we planned for them to churn when their contract came up for renewal in April. Perhaps they've already sent us a cancellation notice in January. Rather than just accepting the loss of $310k of ARR, we might use the months of February and March for our customer success team to work exceptionally hard to fix whatever is going wrong in the account. We might even offer them a one-time discount of 50% to stay with us for one more year to make things right. If successful, we'll have captured $155k of ARR over and above our annual plan.

Similarly, we might have expected that LuminaCore would be so happy with our solution that they'd accept the 6% price increase their contract allowed without any hesitation. We may not have planned to send the invoice until April but received a call from them in January threatening to cancel their contract unless we hold the pricing flat this year. In that instance, we may agree to preserve their contract at $589k, but we'll be missing out on $35k of expansion that was in our annual plan. We can make the best of this situation by trying to negotiate something else into the renewal that works to our advantage—perhaps increasing the automatic renewal term from three to five years or obligating them to participate in a written case study we can use to attract other customers.

As you plan your year, also pay attention to which months will have lots of renewals and which months will have fewer, using those slow times to get ahead of the biggest renewal opportunities that can have the most impact on your annual performance. A chart like the one in Figure 13.2 may be helpful to plan and manage this work. The puts and takes of the various customer situations will be fluid and involve concessions and adaptations from your finance team, customer success team, and other stakeholders. Keeping a structured document of what your plan is, what actually happened, and whether you're ahead or behind on the net retention implications is key.

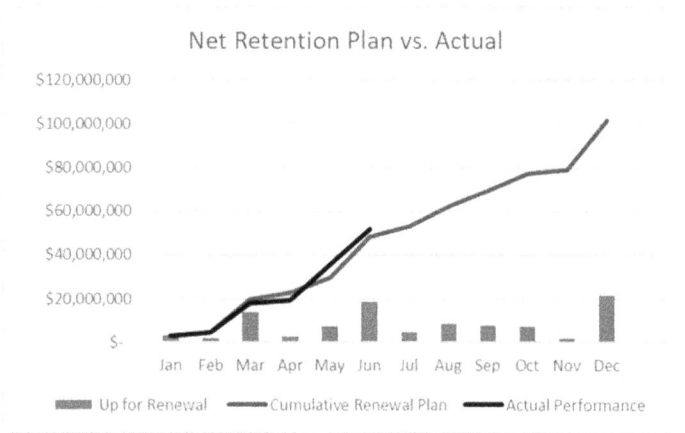

Fig 13.2: Tracking Net Retention Plan vs. Actual Attainment

Bring all the stakeholders together at least monthly, look out to as many months into the future as possible to adjust your plans, and report results to your board with as much importance as you do your new logo wins. Your renewal base is the biggest part of your company's revenue stream. Be sure it's getting managed with the attention it deserves.

CHAPTER 14

Club Trips

———— ⧋ ————

The first time I was invited to a Sales Club trip, I had no idea what it was all about. My company had just been acquired by a bigger one. We were at the annual Sales Kickoff, and I was called up on stage alongside about fifty other sellers who had achieved 100% or more of their quota the year before.

A movie played, showing pictures of white sand beaches and tranquil spa pools, accompanied by island-themed steel drum music. Our CRO announced that each of us would be going on a trip together to stay at the Four Seasons Hotel on an island called Nevis – and we could bring a guest, too.

Every seller on stage was excited. Every seller not on stage was jealous. More than a few sellers Googled "Nevis" and discovered it is in the West Indies. A few of them continued googling to discover that the West Indies is an island region in the Caribbean.

A few weeks before the trip was to happen, I got a package in the mail with a leather-bound itinerary offering three choices of activities each day, including golf, shopping trips, tours of local landmarks, massages, or just lounging by the pool while hotel attendants brought fruity drinks and misted guests with cooling waters. The trip itself beat even these expectations. My partner and I flew to the nearby island of St. Kitts, where a private boat collected us and our luggage at the dock for a half-hour trip to the Four Seasons, where we were given a stack of local currency to spend and led to our room.

Each night brought a dinner more extravagant than the night before. Returning to our room after meals of freshly caught fish, accompanied by a local steel drum band, my guest and I would find a surprise gift waiting for us, including a bag of beachwear and sunscreen, a set of Waterford crystal with a bottle of Champagne, an inflatable boat, local pottery, and more. When it was time to leave, the attendants packed our things into boxes and shipped them home so we wouldn't have to struggle with them on the plane.

We told all of our friends and colleagues about the trip, and my partner started asking how I was doing on my next quota so that we could go on another fantastic trip on the company's dime.

Deciding Whether Club Is Right For Your Company

For sales organizations that have them, trips like this serve as important motivators that drive sellers to achieve great things. They also serve as an important "thank you" to the loved ones who sacrifice to support their high-performing seller, recognizing that great sales performance often involves last-minute cancellation of dinner plans or shortened attendance at kids' birthday parties to accommodate a last-minute cross-country flight to close a deal.

That's why Club trips have become an expected component of overall compensation in some industries, where sellers (and their spouses) ask as many questions about the Club trip as they do the benefits packages before accepting a job offer.

When I began my sales career, social media wasn't yet "a thing." If you weren't on the trip itself, you didn't know much about it, and if you weren't in sales, it was highly unlikely that you were aware that such a trip even occurred. When sellers started photographing moments on these trips (possibly with the smartphone they were gifted at the event) and posting them to social media, more and more colleagues in departments far away from the sales organization started to see them in high-resolution detail.

And they started to ask questions.

"I work really hard at my job. Why don't I get invited to trips like this?" "I thought our company was struggling financially. How are we paying for this extravagance?" "Salespeople already get paid way more than everyone else. Why can't they pay for their own vacation like I do?" "If I didn't write great code, they wouldn't have anything to sell. How is this fair?"

Some organizations responded by explaining and defending that it's a tool to attract top talent to a job that customarily includes it as a benefit. Salespeople are more "at risk" in their jobs than anyone else, much more likely to be fired after a quarter or two of missed quotas than any other employee with inconsistent performance.

Other organizations expanded the trip eligibility to "top performers" from every department across the company.

During years of serious financial pressures (and then again during years of COVID stay-at-home orders), some companies canceled their trips and "forgot to reinstate them" after the storm had passed.

Because of my first experience in Nevis, I'm a huge advocate of Club trips for the informal team-building opportunities they create for the colleagues in attendance and for the motivation, inspiration, and reward they give the best sellers.

As a head of sales, I don't have a particular opinion about whether employees in other departments should be able to qualify for them. Still, I recognize that once you have widened the circle, it will be very hard to shrink again when times get tough. For events to really have the impact you're seeking, they also need to be experiences that the attendees are unlikely to be able to afford or plan on their own. A weekend at an all-inclusive, midrange resort or discount cruise won't do. So, whatever your company decides, make sure you're committed to finding the budget for it every year, forever.

Picking A Location

The trip's destination needs to be something truly inspirational—an experience that your attendees will talk about enthusiastically for years and which will inspire them to work even harder to achieve quota again. Four letter islands (Bali, Fiji, Maui) are popular destinations, as are luxury resorts in global capital cities (Paris, Rome, Sydney). Variety across the years is important so that sellers who qualify multiple years in a row continue to be surprised and delighted with the experience.

Considering the diversity of your employee population is also important. While some of my colleagues traveled to Nevis with a "friend" or "cousin," the country's laws and attitudes about LGBTQ+ people have now eliminated it from the list of destinations I consider when I have a say in trip planning. A proposed trip to a hotel whose rooms circled a dolphin pool raised concerns about the sensibilities of employees who became passionate about animal rights issues surfaced in the movie Blackfish. One very large company I worked for had so many sellers (and qualifiers) that they always offered employees a choice of two trips: an ultra-luxury trip for two or a less-luxurious, family-oriented trip for two adults and two kids.

Whatever the specifics of your situation, be sure that you're choosing a destination that is going to appeal to as many attendees as possible, offend none, and actually be a motivator for future performance.

Some organizations offer employees the choice of a trip or an equivalent cash bonus. I find that option less exciting. Like my sellers, who would prefer a five-foot-tall trophy to a $5k bonus, the cash reward doesn't seem as motivational, especially to the top sellers who have already cashed six or seven-figure commission checks. Taking the cash also eliminates the opportunity to interact with colleagues one-on-one, missing an essential culture-building opportunity.

All Expenses Paid

As you plan your trip, be sure you're planning for every expense to be paid by the company. Every. One. That includes transportation or parking at the employee's home airport, airfare, hotel stay, activity fees, on-trip transportation, meals, tips, and some spending money for souvenirs. For US employees, these are taxable benefits, so also work with your finance team to give the employee an additional cash bonus that is grossed-up to cover all taxes they owe.

To minimize the tax impact, some organizations find ways to have small meetings during the event so that at least a portion becomes a "business expense." Consult your tax professional and your conscience in your planning, and remember that particularly with guests on the trip, this should be more about rewarding hard work than doing more of it.

Timing

Ideally, you are announcing the qualifiers of your trip at your first sales meeting of the year, creating an exciting motivational moment with a video sizzle reel that gets them excited about the adventure they're headed on.

At the same time, you'll want to announce an equally exciting destination that you'll be heading to the following year, giving the sellers in the room who didn't qualify this year something to strive for all year long.

To get maximum benefit from the trip, you'll want to talk about it with the team multiple times during the year. If our Club Trip is a beach destination, I like to mail sellers small vials of sand or seashells with a note that reminds them what they're working for. If it's a ski trip, I might send artificial snow. Sending these notes to their home, where a spouse is likely to see them, adds extra encouragement to beat quota and is another way to create momentum. When my first seller hits 100% of their goal, I'll make a big announcement during a company meeting, giving them an "I'm going to Paris!" beret to wear or something similarly attention-getting.

The trip itself is ideally scheduled for four to six months after the new year. Many sellers who are top performers one year enter the next with little open pipeline, as they pulled out every stop so they could close the prior year strong. Awarding them a trip that they'll have to wait around another few months to go on minimizes the likelihood of them looking for a job at the start of the year. By the time the trip has happened, they'll have already spent a few months re-building their territory and closing a few more deals.

All of these timing considerations and the logistics of planning group travel lead to some long and overlapping calendars of activities. In Q3 of one year, you may be selecting and negotiating a hotel contract for an island-based trip that you'll announce in Q1 of the following year and actually go on in Q2 of the year after that. In the meantime, you're finalizing the details of the gifts and announcing the qualifiers for a global city-based Club trip you'll be attending just before evaluating whether a private yacht-based Club trip would be appealing for the next year.

	Q1	Q2	Q3	Q4
THIS YEAR			Select destination and negotiate Island Club	Finalize details of City Club gifts, attendee list
NEXT YEAR	Announce qualifiers for City Club Announce Island Destination	Attend City Club	Select destination and negotiate Yacht Club	Finalize details of Island Club gifts, attendee list
FOLLOWING YEAR	Announce qualifiers for Island Club Announce Yacht Destination	Attend Island Club		

Fig 14.1: The Intricacies of Club Trip Planning

There are a lot of details to juggle, particularly as you're focused on forecasting the business and leading a team to performance that will allow you to avoid that "gone in under a year and a half" tenure of most sales leaders. The nature of these events also means you're booking hotel rooms almost two years in advance for a set of guests you have no way of naming and are taking a best guess at counting. Having an experienced marketing events team—or even better, a contract with a corporate events planning company that produces these experiences for all sorts of companies all the time—will serve you well.

Who Hosts?

If your Club trip is sales-only, you will likely be the event's named host as CRO. If your trip is company-wide, your CEO's name is likely on all invitations, notes, and awards. In practice, you're likely to have multiple executives in attendance, and all of you have hosting duties during the trip. Prior to traveling, make sure that every executive gets a dossier that includes a list of employees attending, their photo, the name of their guest, and some personal details about their achievements, hobbies, or other facts.

Throughout the trip, make an effort to personally connect with each attendee and their guest, checking off names as you do, and coordinating with your colleagues to track down and identify any that you haven't gotten to speak with yet. These are the personal connections that your employees will remember, and will continue to build loyalty amongst your team.

Professional Behavior

While you are all probably traveling with guests of your own, this is a work trip for your executive team. That may mean participating in a day outing that you might not have preferred in order to have a member of the c-team in attendance at all of the offerings that day, or it might mean making one more trip to the pool when you'd rather just go to your room to take a nap.

The Club trip provides even more unscripted social interaction time than an in-person Sales Kickoff, often with alcohol and swimwear in the mix. Be sure you continue to maintain an impeccable, unimpeachable executive reputation. Gently remind your employees about the importance of staying within professional behavior limits even as they relax together. These are your top performers, the ones you most want to keep in the company. Don't let anyone mess it up.

CHAPTER 15

Preparing for the Exit

If you work in a PE-backed company, you will eventually have to start planning for your current investor's "exit."

Understanding the PE lifecycle can be confusing for those who have never gone through the process before. I often explain it to friends and family as something like flipping a house. First, the PE firm buys a company that seems to have good "bones" but which they know they can improve on.

Then, like replacing the house's kitchen or remodeling the lower level, they work with the company over a period of years to make it even more valuable by executing a "value creation plan." This might be an additional investment in growth, the launch of a new product, mergers and acquisitions, cost-cutting measures, or some combination of all of the above. As CRO, you play an important part in this renovation work.

Finally, the PE firm exits the business when it believes it can get a good return on its investment. It often aims for a sales price of two, three, or more times what it bought it for, often on a four- to five-year time horizon.

As a key leader in the business, you should have some "equity" in the company as an owner alongside the PE firm, and you'll also have a financial incentive to help them achieve a good exit.

Helping to prepare your company for sale can often feel like a full-time job in itself. The process involves a few steps:

Preparation and Planning

Throughout the time the PE firm owns your company (the "hold period"), they will periodically evaluate the company's current financial performance, market position, growth prospect, potential buyer interest, and estimated current value. A common metric of company health is whether it is a "Rule of 40" company. At different times, the market may value growth over EBITDA—or the reverse—but achieving "Rule of 40" though any path is usually highly prized.

Company valuation, or the price a buyer will pay for the company, is generally calculated as a multiple of one-year EBITDA or total ARR. Healthier companies command higher multiples, a key negotiation point in the final sale.

Engaging Advisors

As you get close to a sale, your PE firm usually hires investment bankers and other advisors to assist with the sale process. Like a realtor selling your home, these advisors prepare marketing materials, identify potential buyers, manage negotiations, and provide strategic guidance.

A key part of their work will be to prepare a Confidential Information Presentation (CIP). This is like the marketing brochure that describes the number of rooms in your house, pictures of the backyard, and so on. CIPs are generally written in PowerPoint and can run over a hundred pages long, including details on the products you sell, their marketing messages, the competitive landscape, total addressable market, details about your revenues, customer retention statistics, org charts, bios of your executive team, and more. Remembering that the next buyer may be another PE firm that wants to add value of their own, the CIP may include additional suggestions on where investments may be spent on the next Value Creation Plan run under their watch.

As CRO, you may be a key person these teams rely on to collect information and build the CIP. It is traditional to assign a codename to your sale, both to limit the likelihood that employees will see your calendar filled up with "selling the company" appointments and also to further protect confidential information when it is discussed by potential investors. Codenames take their inspiration from all sorts of things—songs, sports teams, landmarks, mythical creatures, and more—so you may find yourself talking with colleagues about something like "Project Rhumba" to discuss these activities.

Marketing and Buyer Outreach

Armed with the CIP, your advisors will begin circulating it (under NDA) to potential buyers. These may include "strategic buyers" (who are competitors or companies in related industries that might want to purchase your company) and "financial" or "strategic" buyers (who are other PE firms). If you are large enough, you may also consider going live on the stock exchange through an Initial Public Offering (IPO), but that process is outside the scope of what I'm describing here.

Initial Bids and Due Diligence

Potential buyers will submit a non-binding, preliminary bid based on the information they read in your CIP. The PE firm and its advisors will then select a shortlist of potential bidders from those submitted and allow them to participate in additional "due diligence." Here, the potential buyers request additional, more detailed information about the company to verify the information in the CIP and arrive at their own assessment of potential risks, opportunities, and value-creation plans.

You should expect to be asked to provide written responses to detailed questions alongside other reports and data that you share with potential buyers in secure, online "virtual data rooms." You will probably also participate in group presentations and interviews with various audiences. Sometimes, this is referred to as "going on a road show," as you largely present the same pitch over and over to multiple audiences.

Final Bids and Negotiation

Through these conversations, a single buyer will begin to emerge as your preferred buyer. Like buying a house, it may not be the person who bid the highest. Other elements of the offer might distinguish them, including how quickly they are willing to close the deal, how much debt will be involved in the transaction (your company will likely be stuck with the interest payments after the deal is done), whether they intend to keep the same leadership team in place or replace you with their own team, cultural synergies, and many more items.

It is typical for that bidder to submit a more binding "Letter of Intent" and to ask for an "exclusivity period" during which they are the only buyer you are negotiating with and providing final "confirmatory" diligence to arrive at a final, binding contract to purchase your company. You should expect to be involved in additional conversations, supporting your team during this confirmatory phase of negotiation.

Closing and Transition

Once a buyer is chosen, the final terms of the sale are documented in a definitive agreement. Depending on your industry, there may be regulatory reviews and government agencies examining the deal to ensure that it doesn't run afoul of anti-monopoly rules or other financial regulations.

During this time, it is important that you adhere to a set of rules that your legal counsel is likely to provide you. Particularly if you are being sold to a strategic buyer, you need to take special care not to do certain transitional work until after the deal is closed, as things like planning for the marketing or pricing of your products with a soon-to-be-owner-but-current-competitor may run afoul of price fixing or other laws.

Post-close, you should be prepared for any number of personal and professional outcomes. Your deal with the buyer may have been contingent on you agreeing to work at the new company for some prescribed length of time, but you may learn they don't want you to do so shortly after the closing date.

Some deals will offer you an opportunity to "roll over" part or all of your equity from the old company into the new company or to co-invest your own money into the new business. Some deals are contingent on key executives rolling over some investment or other similar terms. Remember that during these negotiations, your company's legal counsel represents the company's interest – not yours – and so you may want to have your own attorney review terms and make sure you understand what commitments you're making and what guarantees you are or are not getting in return before signing documents.

Rules and regulations regarding executive compensation change often. Expect that you may suddenly need to make additional agreements with various parties to make sure your deal is complying with "golden parachute" laws or restructure other deal terms to be as tax efficient as possible.

Continuing to Manage Your Team

As you complete the exit, know that your experience of the transaction may be very different from that of your direct employees. As a company executive, you likely are receiving an equity check that is larger than any paycheck you've ever received in your life. That may make it less painful if your employment is suddenly terminated post-close, or you may have already determined with the new owner that you won't be continuing on to the new company. It's also possible that you'll continue in your role, chasing another exit for the new owner in another few years.

Your front line sellers, though, are probably not receiving any such windfall and are likely to be worried about what the new ownership structure means for their jobs. If you've made good use of your project codename and kept confidentiality tightly, employees may not even know that the company was up for sale until the day the transaction is finalized and there's an all-company meeting (or press release) to announce it.

Whatever your circumstance, remember that your primary responsibility as CRO (for whatever time you have remaining in the role) is to maximize the revenues of your company, which means continuing to motivate and inspire your sellers to continue working to their best potential.

This means continuing to hold forecasting calls and Deal Clinics, assisting with key sales opportunities, and likely even more individual engagement with nervous employees looking for clear and transparent communication about whatever concerns or rumors are being passed around.

It is common for employees to search for new jobs and voluntarily quit the company in the months following an exit transaction—even the ones you hoped would stay—because of the fear, uncertainty, and doubt of the new situation. Do your best to stay close to your team members and prevent this from happening.

Do all of this as you privately process your own fears and concerns about your new role and colleagues and work with them on the plans and transitions to whatever your new company strategy will become.

CHAPTER 16

Leaving Professionally

A successful PE exit may include you leaving your CRO role, whether you want to or not. You may also find yourself leaving the company outside the timing of a transaction, sometimes by your own choosing and sometimes not.

Regardless of the circumstances, it is important to conduct a professional exit. The executive community is small, and the private equity community is even smaller. Your actions in your exit from a company are likely to make the conversational rounds in this highly connected network, and your resulting professional reputation will directly impact whatever is next in your professional career.

Begin the process by reviewing your executive employment agreement. It likely already outlines a number of obligations you have to your employer regarding notice periods, transitional support, and other activities during and after your employment ends. Be sure you're familiar with all of them and are prepared to meet or exceed the minimum expectations described. This may be a great time to reconnect with your personal attorney to remind you of what you must, can, and can't do in the coming months or years.

Whether you're leaving what you saw as a toxic work environment, have been surprised by a sudden dismissal, are elated to move on after an extremely successful PE exit, or are being recruited to a new role you're intrigued and excited about, your emotions may cloud your thinking. A dispassionate legal advisor can help you see through all of it and make the right choices.

Managed Communications

When you are leaving of your own volition, let your direct supervisor (likely the CEO) be the first person you share the news with. Then, no matter how desperately you want to talk to others, let them take the lead on who is in the know and when.

Expect that they may soon involve a Chief Human Resources Officer, board members, or a PR team in a "circle of trust" to talk about your imminent departure. In all instances, commit to letting this group lead on building a communications plan that involves who is told when, what the message is, and what channels it will be communicated through. Building your exit communication may take days or weeks to put together. During this time, continue to lead your teams as normal (unless instructed otherwise). Besides your spouse and personal legal counsel, do not tell anyone else your news. Not your favorite lieutenant, not your best friend on the c-team, nobody.

When you're allowed to share the news, stick to whatever message has been agreed to with your CEO and leadership team. No matter how excited you may be to announce your new role or how desperately you want to confide in someone about how terribly you think you're being treated, you must keep these comments to yourself.

It's become cliché to say that an executive has decided that they want to spend more time with an aging parent or taking the "opportunity to be a parent to my pre-teen kid, which only comes once in a lifetime." So long as you're not being asked to break laws or severely violate common rules of ethics and decency, stick to the script – in public, in private, on LinkedIn and other social media, in meetings with your direct reports and extended sales team, and in company meetings. Everywhere and always.

Prepare A Great Transition

With whatever time you have, prepare a dossier of key information your successor may find useful. Perhaps you already know who this is. Perhaps a search hasn't yet begun, and your replacement won't arrive until long after you've left. Regardless of the situation, give your successor the information you think they need to know to pick up successfully where you've left off.

This likely includes information about deals in flight, profiles of key customers, and forecasting information for your current month, quarter, and year. You should also provide a calendar of upcoming meetings, events, and future commitments that need coverage, along with any details someone else might find useful as they step into your shoes.

As tedious as you may find it, you should write performance reviews for each of your direct reports up to the date of your departure, giving them a written copy that they can share with their new manager when the annual review process comes around. You should include these reviews in a file for your successor, alongside other observations about your extended sales team, such as key individuals who are high performers, low performers, flight risks, and more. Update your Talent Nine Block. While you leave the organization and the new leader may reject all of your advice, share your perspective on likely interim and long-term successors who can fill different roles as needed.

It's a lot of material to put together. That's why most executive transitions are agreed to take at least a month rather than the two weeks that are customary for lower-level employees. Be sure you're putting your best effort into assembling this documentation regardless of your enthusiasm for the task.

Icing on the Cake

At the end of his first term as President, George Bush lost a hard-fought election to Bill Clinton, who promised to push very different priorities than Bush did as President. On the day of his transition, President Bush left President Clinton a note in the Oval Office which read (in part):

> "I wish you great happiness here … There will be very tough times, made even more difficult by criticism you may not think is fair. I'm not a very good one to give advice; but just don't let the critics discourage you or push you off course.

> You will be <u>our</u> President when you read this note. I wish you well. I wish your family well.

> Your success now is our country's success. I am rooting hard for you."

I've always found this to be a classy note to a successor, one that recognizes that they're in a very small group of people who understand the particular challenges and nuances of the role they onced filled.

Depending on the terms of your separation, you may retain equity in the company long after you're gone. In this way, like President Bush, you have a vested interest in seeing your successor do well in the role—regardless of whether you think they will do it the way you would have done.

I've found that when I take the time to send my own successors a heartfelt note that genuinely wishes them success, offering to be a resource to them if they ever need it at any time in the future, I've never been disappointed by the result.

Continuing to be a cheerleader for them, for their team, and the company you left in private—and in public on LinkedIn and elsewhere—distinguishes you as a truly classy professional. While this reputation may open doors for you in the future, its true value lies in the positive impact it has on your professional relationships and personal growth.

Complete the Administrative Details

There are countless little things that may need to be unwound to fully detach from your company, such as:

- Returning keys to offices, alongside any copies you have of confidential company information, laptops and other company equipment.

- Executing paperwork to remove you from bank accounts or company credit cards.

- Surrendering club memberships or resigning from industry associations.

- Canceling your use of company Uber accounts, and more.

- Signing a separation agreement that reiterates obligations from your employment agreement, and provides the details of final paychecks, treatments of your equity positions, and other topics.

Like your work in preparing for a great transition, you should give proper care and attention to the details of each of these and complete them as quickly as possible without requiring your former employer to chase you down for them.

You're likely excited about whatever you'll do next, whether it be a challenging new role or a family vacation. You'll be able to enjoy them even more fully when you don't have these final tasks hanging over your head.

Tie Relationships With a Bow

When you leave your role, you're leaving behind a network of team members who contributed to your success. When appropriate, thank them individually without making it seem like you're trying to hold on to some professional/management role after your departure. Write heartfelt endorsements on LinkedIn, and let them know you're always available to help them in any way you can while steering clear of any actions that might violate a non-solicitation or non-disparagement agreement you may have in place.

If you've done a great job for your PE firm, they likely want to stay in touch with you, too, even after they've sold off the investment. Investors love to invest in proven quantities – and if you did well for them at one company, you'd likely be on a shortlist of folks they want to talk to when they need a CRO at another one, too; no long and expensive recruiting processes needed.

By maintaining solid relationships even after leaving a company, I've had the opportunity to be offered jobs to work with colleagues again in multiple contexts. I'm honored that I have some team members who have accepted roles on my team at two and three different companies across our careers. I have an even wider network of folks that I can turn to for advice on a wide variety of professional topics because I've maintained these relationships. They've been great returns on small investments in human connection. And they just make professional life better.

CHAPTER 17

Advocating for Yourself

Following a successful tenure as CRO for a PE-backed company, many professionals repeat the experience by going to another one. With one experience under their belt, they're often much more educated about pitfalls to watch out for in negotiating their next role.

Yet even for the experienced CRO, a single experience is just that—a single experience. And while lower-level employees may be able to check the details of their agreement against similar roles at other companies—or even their own company—on sites like Salary.com or Glassdoor, benchmarking information across the executive level is much less available – often only hinted at, or whispered between very close colleagues or recruiters who have their own incentives and agendas.

This chapter aims to accelerate your path on that learning curve, orienting you to the key terms to pay attention to when negotiating your employment agreement, even if it's your first time doing so. If you've never worked with an employment attorney before, your first role as a CRO is a great time to start. Executive contracts are often much more complex than the one- or two-page offer letter agreements you may have seen as a frontline seller, and it's helpful to have someone advising you who has seen a wide variety of similar agreements in the past. Expect to pay a few thousand dollars for an attorney's assistance in this process. Given the potential dollars at play in the various potential facets of your executive compensation, you will recoup this investment many times over in a well-crafted agreement.

In reading this chapter, please recognize that it is meant to orient you to the different types of terms you may find in a common agreement, but you are unlikely to find all of them in yours. Different PE firms have different standard contracts for their executive teams, and those more generous to you in one area are likely to be less generous in others. This collection of terms represents some of the better and worse variations of terms that may or may not be offered to you in your role as CRO.

The Basics

First, expect the basics that companies promote on their websites and job postings. This includes 401k plans, vacation days, medical and dental insurance—all of these standard benefits should be documented in your executive employment agreement.

You should also expect cash compensation, generally 50% in base salary and 50% in variable compensation. Your variable compensation may include a straight commission on every dollar the company sells in a year, a bonus tied to hitting certain EBITDA or growth targets, or some combination of the two.

Try to negotiate variable pay to be targeted at achievement of the company-documented annual plan (the Board Plan), not the higher-level targets represented by the 10% or 20% inflation you've added to the quotas of individual members of your team. You may not get all the way there, but the less padding you have on the company plan, the better. Getting accelerated payouts for overperformance is also a great term to ask for.

The timing of variable pay may be longer than that of your front-line sellers. While it's great to get monthly payouts, you may need to settle for quarterly, semi-annually, or even annual bonus payments. Regardless of the timing, ensure that you will be paid for all bonuses earned even if you're no longer employed by the company. A CRO who only worked at the company for half the year may only be entitled to half their bonus.

They may have to wait until the payment is made to everyone else six months after their departure, but it should be paid in recognition of the work they did to contribute to the result.

Unlike most employees, you may not see cost of living salary adjustments year to year. PE-backed employers believe that you're always within four or five years of an exit that should have a significant equity payout for you, which more than compensates for the average 3% increase available to non-executives.

The Equity

One of the key benefits of working for a company owned by private equity is the opportunity to be an equity holder in the business yourself.

CROs in B2B tech companies are typically offered equity grants that represent between .75% and 1.5% ownership of the entire company, though actual experiences vary wildly. These grants typically vest over a defined period of time, usually four to five years, and it isn't unusual to have to wait a year before the first bit of equity is vested.

For example, a common agreement might specify that "equity vests across five years with a one-year cliff," after which it accrues on a quarterly basis. In such an example, the CRO has not vested in any equity until their one-year anniversary, at which point they are 20% vested. One quarter later, they'll vest in another 5% for a total of 25% and keep earning 5% more each quarter until their five-year anniversary – at which point they are 100% vested.

Variations in vesting may exist that require your company to achieve certain financial objectives for vesting to occur, or have some portion of equity vesting with these requirements while another portion accrues strictly by time.

Some agreements may provide a term to accelerate all unvested equity upon a "change in control" (i.e., reaching the PE exit early). In contrast, others may suggest that such accelerated vesting will be left up to the discretion of the PE firm and board involved. It can feel scary to trust that this will happen if not explicitly called out in your agreement, but the common wisdom is that any PE firm that fails to "do the right thing" will get a bad reputation in the industry and find it difficult to recruit any executives to work for their portfolios in the future.

The vesting term is non-negotiable in your agreement and is generally the same for every member of the executive team. Nevertheless, it's important for you to understand how it works in your specific situation, as it is likely the biggest component of your overall compensation package.

There may be times when you can invest your own money in the business. Consult your financial professional for advice. You may already have so much at play in your granted equity that you'd be taking on undue additional risk by having your day-to-day salary and your own invested money contingent on the same company's value.

At the same time, there may be an unwritten expectation that you make a nominal investment in the business as a show of good faith in their success (and to allow your team to say, "every executive is a personal investor in the company"). At the time of exit, there may be similar expectations that you "roll forward" some of your equity to the next investment, particularly if you are continuing in your role or received that equity as part of an accelerated vesting schedule on change in control.

In all of these equity situations, CROs in the US may need to complete paperwork to prove they are an "accredited investor." This tells the Securities and Exchange Commission that they meet certain income or net worth criteria that help them bear the risk of being invested in a complex or risky security, like shares in a company owned by private equity, for which no market may exist to sell when you want to. Generally, your income as

CRO will help you overcome this hurdle, though your legal and finance teams can help you find alternate solutions if needed.

In the US, you may also be required to file tax forms to ensure that your equity grant receives preferable tax treatment as long-term capital gains rather than regular income. Your tax professional can advise on the appropriate paperwork and timing requirements. Do not be late in filing these documents!

Companies outside the US have various reporting requirements for these packages. On more than one occasion, I've been surprised by employees who have researched my equity position in London's Companies House and then shared their opinions on it with me and others.

Severance Benefits

As a key executive, it is in your company's interest for you to stay in your job – even when things aren't going well. In fact, a company that is troubled has even more need for you to stay in your CRO role, putting all of your efforts into righting the ship. Because they don't want to be in a situation where you see things going badly, search for a new job, and leave because you're worried about being laid off or fired, your employment agreement may provide for certain severance benefits in the event that the company terminates your employment.

Like a prenuptial agreement, these benefits are best negotiated at the beginning of your relationship when you like each other the most rather than as part of a bitter separation when things have started to go poorly. Benefits associated with an involuntary separation may include:

- Continuation of your salary for a period of time after termination (typically between 6 and 12 months)

- Continuation of your health insurance and other benefits for the same period

- Ownership of your vested equity at the time of separation. Some companies may choose to pay out your vested equity at whatever value they determined it to be on your termination date, while others will allow you to leave the equity invested in the company until they reach their next exit – at which point it will be paid out at the exit value. Some companies may take your preferences into consideration when making this decision.

To qualify for these benefits, your company may require your termination to be "not for cause" or one that did not happen under "negative circumstances." The definition of these terms is often highly negotiated and documented in your employment agreement. Negative circumstances that may lead to your forfeiture of these benefits may include:

- Being convicted of a felony

- Committing an act of moral turpitude (this, too, is a legally-defined term)

- Violating the rules and regulations of your company in a material way. Your agreement may also include a provision that allows you to be notified of the violation in writing and given a 30-day period to "cure" the violation before it triggers forfeiture of benefits).

If you choose to resign your position, you generally forfeit all severance benefits except those associated with vested equity so long as you provide sufficient notice (generally one to two months) and participate in a constructive transition process. However, there may be circumstances where you quit "for good reason" and would be entitled to all of the benefits. Such "good reasons" may include:

- Your job duties or salary have been significantly diminished

- You are being asked to violate a law

- You are being asked to move your primary place of employment more than a certain number of miles

- You have become mentally or physically incapacitated or unable to perform your job

- You have died (in which case, your heirs are entitled to your severance benefits)

In a mirror of involuntary separation benefits, you may be required to notify the company in writing of your "good reasons" and provide them a 30-day period in which to "cure" the issue at hand.

Obligations after Separation

Whether your separation was voluntary or involuntary, you may have a variety of obligations to your former employer. These include:

- Agreeing not to work for a competitor for a defined period of time (non-compete agreement)

- Agreeing not to hire employees away from the employer for a defined period (non-solicitation agreement)

- Agreeing not to encourage any customers to terminate their contracts with your former employer.

- Agreeing not to speak negatively about the company or its employees or products (non-disparagement agreement). You should request that this be reciprocal and potentially pre-negotiate a positive reference from your employer post-separation (while recognizing that the PE world is very tight-knit, and negative sentiment about you may get around no matter what the agreement says).

- Agreeing to support the employer in future litigation for which you may have expertise (ex., assisting in their defense in claims of copyright violation or certain employee lawsuits). In such instances, your employer should pay your reasonable expenses and reasonable compensation for your time.

Other Terms

Your employment agreement is likely to include other terms that define:

- Who owns the copyright to any inventions you produce while employed at the company

- Expense reimbursement policies, including types of expenses covered and timeframe for repayment

- What is considered confidential information of the company, and how should to be treated

- Who can know the details of your employment agreement (generally only your spouse, attorney, and financial advisor)

- The processes you'll use to resolve any number of unique circumstances that may arise over the course of your employment

CHAPTER 18

Leadership and Culture

———— ⚬ ————

I hope the strategies, tactics, and templates I've shared here give you a solid framework for building a successful sales organization. However, true high performance isn't achieved through processes and templates alone. It's fueled by the intangible forces of leadership and culture and entire books have been written on these topics.

As a CRO, your ability to cultivate a positive, motivating, and high-achieving culture is just as crucial as your ability to set quotas and create reliable forecasts.

With my history of operation in PE environments, my decades of work in tech companies, and my academic background in the social sciences, I've come to describe my leadership style as one that exists at the intersection of business, technology, and humanity. I get most excited about work that lets me explore the tradeoffs, conflicts, and synergies that are at play when two or more of those issues collide.

Your leadership style will be unique to your personal strengths, experiences, and worldviews. Whether you can articulate it in a pithy tagline or not, your leadership style and behavior—right down to the color of your shoes—will permeate the culture in which your teams operate.

The CRO as a Culture Catalyst

That's why a CRO isn't just someone who brings money into the business; they're a culture catalyst. The tone you set, the values you embody, and the behaviors you reward will permeate your team and shape its culture. A positive culture fosters collaboration, innovation, and a shared commitment to success. It attracts and retains top talent, fuels motivation, and drives exceptional results.

A three-Legged Stool of Values

As the leader of a large sales team, I know that my team members will inevitably face countless decisions and situations I'll never be privy to. To ensure they make the right choices—even in my absence—it's crucial to establish a strong foundation of shared values and communicate and reinforce them regularly.

When everyone operates from the same core principles, I can trust their judgment and support their decisions regardless of the outcome, and be proud of the organization I work with and lead. That's why I include a question about the core values the candidate brings to their job in every interview I conduct, and I scrutinize the answer closely to make sure their values are compatible with my own.

For my teams, I've distilled my values down to three key ideas that every member should hold:

Integrity

We conduct ourselves with honesty, transparency, and ethical behavior in all interactions, both internally and externally. The temptation to cut corners or engage in unethical practices for short-term gains can be strong in sales. However, the long-term consequences for both personal and company reputation far outweigh any fleeting benefits. I regularly remind my sellers that tech sales is a tight-knit world, and their reputation will precede them across many different organizations. No short-term commission check is worth risking that long-term reputation.

Respect

We treat each other, our customers, and our partners with respect, empathy, and compassion. While we may challenge each other and our clients to make the best decisions, we do so with kindness and understanding. Nobody enjoys working with a jerk, and a positive, supportive environment fosters collaboration and long-term success.

Results

We are driven to achieve exceptional results, consistently exceeding expectations and delivering on our commitments. At the end of the day, we're all here to achieve a goal, and in sales, that goal is clearly measurable. We strive for excellence and hold ourselves accountable for delivering results.

Fig 18.1: The Three Value Pillars of My Culture and Leadership Style

These values aren't just aspirational ideals but the bedrock of my team's culture. They operate like a three-legged stool: all three legs must be solidly present in equal measure to stand strong. A seller who consistently delivers outstanding results but treats colleagues or clients poorly undermines the team's morale and jeopardizes long-term success and won't be on my team for very long, no matter how much quota they retire. Conversely, a kind and well-intentioned seller who consistently misses their targets isn't contributing to the team's overall goals and won't have a long-term place in the organization, either.

These values aren't just discussed on day one; they're woven into every aspect of my work. I revisit these values regularly in team meetings, one-on-ones, and performance reviews, and I encourage team members to use them as a guide for decision-making and behavior whenever they have a choice between two paths forward.

Living Values Beyond the Sales Team

While these values are crucial within the sales team, their impact extends beyond our department. As a CRO, you're part of the executive leadership team, and your interactions with your c-suite peers significantly influence the overall company culture.

Just as you wouldn't tolerate a top-performing salesperson who mistreats their colleagues, you shouldn't tolerate disrespectful or unethical behavior from other departments and they shouldn't tolerate it from you, either.

Just as our SMarketing culture tries to break down the barriers between sales and marketing teams, we also need to advocate for a culture of collaboration, respect, and shared accountability across the rest of the organization. This includes the finance team that processes our commission checks, the legal teams that review our contracts, the development teams that build the products we sell, the HR teams that support our employees, and beyond. Cultivating a positive and supportive environment—even when other c-team members aren't ready to do so—benefits everyone, fostering innovation, productivity, and, ultimately, company-wide success.

Conclusion

The journey we've taken together through the pages of this book has been a deep dive into the world of the CRO in a private equity-backed company. We've explored the strategies, tactics, and mindsets that can transform a sales leader from good to exceptional, from achieving targets to exceeding them, from managing a team to inspiring one.

The path of a CRO is not always smooth. It's filled with challenges, setbacks, and moments of doubt. But it's also a path filled with immense opportunities for growth, impact, and reward. By embracing the principles and practices outlined in this book, you're equipping yourself to navigate this path with confidence, resilience, and a relentless focus on success.

Remember that the role of a CRO is not just about hitting numbers in any way possible. It's about building a high-performing sales organization that consistently delivers predictable results. It's about fostering a culture of collaboration, innovation, and continuous improvement. It's about empowering your team to reach their full potential and achieve their personal and professional goals.

As you embark on your journey as a CRO or continue to refine your skills in this role, keep these key takeaways in mind:

Build a solid foundation: Start with a well-defined annual plan, balanced territories, and a clear compensation structure that incentivizes the right behaviors.

Foster collaboration: Break down silos between sales and marketing, creating a unified SMarketing culture that drives lead generation and revenue growth.

Invest in talent: Assess, recruit, and develop your team, providing them with the tools, training, and support they need to succeed.

Embrace data-driven decision-making: Use forecasting, performance metrics, and analytics to gain insights, identify opportunities, and make informed decisions.

Communicate effectively: Build strong relationships with your board, executive team, and employees, fostering trust and transparency.

Prepare for the exit: Understand the private equity lifecycle and actively contribute to the value creation plan, positioning the company for a successful exit.

Leave professionally: When the time comes to move on, do so with grace, integrity, and a commitment to a smooth transition.

Advocate for yourself: Negotiate your employment agreement with confidence, ensuring that your compensation and benefits reflect your value and contributions.

Above all, remember that leadership is not just about achieving results; it's about inspiring and empowering others to achieve greatness. As a CRO, you have the opportunity to make a lasting impact on your company, your team, and your own career. Embrace this opportunity with passion, dedication, and a commitment to excellence.

The journey may be challenging, but the rewards are immeasurable.

Acknowledgements

My sales career has been a humbling one, filled with many triumphs, and as many or more disappointing setbacks. I acknowledge that my journey is far from over, and hope the lessons I've learned and shared so far will give you a fast foundation to becoming a better CRO than I've ever been.

The insights and strategies shared in this book are not solely my own; they're the culmination of years of experience shaped by the wisdom and guidance of many individuals who have played a pivotal role in my growth.

I extend my deepest gratitude to mentors who invested their time and energy in me – even when it wasn't their job to do so and even when I was slow to absorb their lessons.

I'm thankful for each of the managers who chose to hire me on their teams and who generously shared their knowledge and expertise through their own unique styles and cultures. You have served as invaluable examples of what sales leadership can look like.

I'm also grateful to the employers and private equity firms that entrusted me with the leadership and mentorship of their sales teams, giving me the opportunity to put theory into practice and achieve real-world, high-stakes outcomes. I'm honored by your confidence in my abilities and continually motivated by our shared pursuit of significant accomplishments.

Of course, I owe a tremendous debt of gratitude to the thousands of sellers and SMarketers who have worked tirelessly, even during times when my leadership may have faltered. Their dedication, passion, and unwavering commitment to achieving results have been an inspiration. I've learned as much from them as they have from me, and I'm honored to have had the opportunity to work alongside such talented and resilient professionals.

Index

www.ingramcontent.com/pod-product-compliance
Lightning Source LLC
Chambersburg PA
CBHW070657190326

41458CB00053B/6921/J